The Complete

Atkins
Diet Cookbook
2024

Tasteful, High-Fat Recipes Will Revolutionize Your Eating Behaviors for Long-Term Weight Loss and Improved Health

Malte Julia

TABLE OF CONTENTS

Breakfast Recipes

1. Cheesy Spinach Omelette

Total Time: 15 minutes

Cooking Time: 10 minutes

Serves: 1

Ingredients:

- 3 large eggs
- 1 cup fresh spinach, chopped
- 1/4 cup shredded cheddar cheese
- Salt and pepper to taste

Instructions:

1. In a bowl, whisk together eggs and add pepper and salt to taste.
2. A nonstick pan should be heated to medium heat.
3. Cook the spinach in the pan until it wilts.
4. Scatter the spinach with the whisked eggs and cheese.
5. Fold the omelette in half after cooking until the edges are firm.

2. Avocado and Bacon Breakfast Bowl

Total Time: 20 minutes

Cooking Time: 15 minutes

Serves: 2

Ingredients:

- 2 avocados, diced
- 4 slices bacon, cooked and crumbled
- 4 eggs, poached
- Salt and pepper to taste

Instructions:

1. Arrange avocado slices in dishes.
2. Add some crumbled bacon and poached eggs on top.
3. Add pepper and salt for seasoning.

3. Sausage and Egg Muffins

Total Time: 25 minutes

Cooking Time: 20 minutes

Serves: 4

Ingredients:

- 8 eggs
- 8 breakfast sausage patties
- 4 English muffins, split and toasted
- Salt and pepper to taste

Instructions:

1. Follow the directions on the package to cook the sausage patties.
2. Add salt and pepper to scrambled eggs in a different pan.
3. Put toasted English muffins, sausage, and eggs on a sandwich.

4. Keto Pancakes

Total Time: 15 minutes

Cooking Time: 10 minutes

Serves: 2

Ingredients:

- 2/3 cup almond flour
- 2 eggs
- 1/4 cup unsweetened almond milk
- 1 tsp baking powder
- Butter for cooking

Instructions:

1. In a bowl, combine almond flour, eggs, almond milk, and baking powder.

2. Melt butter in a pan over medium heat.

3. Pour the batter into the pan, let it to bubble for a few minutes, then turn it over and continue cooking.

5. Creamy Scrambled Eggs with Smoked Salmon

Total Time: 15 minutes

Cooking Time: 10 minutes

Serves: 2

Ingredients:

- 6 eggs
- 1/4 cup heavy cream

- 4 oz smoked salmon, chopped
- Chives for garnish
- Salt and pepper to taste

Instructions:

1. Beat together eggs and heavy cream; add pepper and salt to taste.
2. In a pan over medium heat, scramble the eggs.
3. Add the smoked salmon and sprinkle the chives over top.

6. Greek Yogurt Parfait

Total Time: 10 minutes

Serves: 1

Ingredients:

- 1 cup Greek yogurt
- 1/2 cup mixed berries
- 1 tbsp chia seeds
- 1 tbsp chopped nuts

Instructions:

1. In a glass or bowl, arrange Greek yogurt, nuts, chia seeds, and berries.

7. Zucchini and Feta Frittata

Total Time: 30 minutes

Cooking Time: 20 minutes

Serves: 4

Ingredients:

- 6 eggs
- 1 zucchini, thinly sliced
- 1/2 cup crumbled feta cheese
- 1/4 cup chopped fresh basil
- Salt and pepper to taste

Instructions:

1. Beat eggs and add pepper and salt to taste.
2. Add eggs, feta, and basil to a baking dish that has been oiled.
3. Bake until golden brown and set.

8. Low-Carb Breakfast Burritos

Total Time: 25 minutes

Cooking Time: 15 minutes

Serves: 2

Ingredients:

- 4 large eggs
- 1/2 cup diced bell peppers
- 1/4 cup diced onions
- 4 low-carb tortillas
- 1/2 cup shredded cheese
- Salsa for topping

Instructions:

1. Add onions and bell peppers to scrambled eggs.

2. Transfer onto tortillas, sprinkle with cheese, and roll up to form burritos.

3. In a skillet over medium heat, melt cheese.

4. Accompany with salsa.

9. Cauliflower Hash Browns

Total Time: 30 minutes

Cooking Time: 20 minutes

Serves: 4

Ingredients:

- 2 cups grated cauliflower
- 2 eggs
- 1/4 cup almond flour
- 1/4 cup grated Parmesan cheese
- Salt and pepper to taste

Instructions:

1. Add the eggs, Parmesan, almond flour, and grated cauliflower.

2. Shape into burgers and sear in a pan until well done.

10. Bacon-Wrapped Egg Cups

Total Time: 25 minutes

Cooking Time: 15 minutes

Serves: 4

Ingredients:

- 8 slices bacon
- 8 eggs
- Salt and pepper to taste
- Chopped chives for garnish

Instructions:

1. Turn the oven on to 375°F, or 190°C.
2. Place bacon slices inside the muffin cups.
3. Add a little salt and pepper to each cup and crack one egg into it.
4. Bake until eggs are set and bacon is crispy.
5. Before serving, garnish with finely chopped chives.

11. Keto Chia Seed Pudding

Total Time: 5 minutes (plus overnight chilling)

Serves: 2

Ingredients:

- 1/4 cup chia seeds
- 1 cup unsweetened almond milk
- 1 tsp vanilla extract
- Stevia or erythritol to taste
- Berries for topping

Instructions:

1. In a jar, combine chia seeds, sugar, almond milk, and vanilla essence.

2. Store in the fridge all night.

3. Drizzle with berries to serve.

12. Egg and Bacon Breakfast Wrap

Total Time: 15 minutes

Cooking Time: 10 minutes

Serves: 1

Ingredients:

- 2 large eggs

- 2 slices bacon

- 1 low-carb tortilla

- 1/4 cup shredded cheese

- Salsa for topping

Instructions:

1. Cook eggs in a pan with bacon until scrambled.

2. Transfer onto a tortilla, top with cheese, and wrap.

3. Add salsa on top.

13. Cottage Cheese and Walnut Bowl

Total Time: 10 minutes

Serves: 1

Ingredients:

- 1 cup cottage cheese

- 1/4 cup chopped walnuts

- 1 tsp honey (optional)
- Cinnamon for sprinkling

Instructions:

1. In a bowl, combine cottage cheese and walnuts.
2. Sprinkle with cinnamon and drizzle with honey.

14. Keto-friendly Smoothie Bowl

Total Time: 10 minutes

Serves: 1

Ingredients:

- 1/2 avocado
- 1/2 cup unsweetened almond milk
- 1/2 cup spinach
- 1/4 cup frozen berries
- 1 tbsp chia seeds

Instructions:

1. Smoothly blend avocado, berries, spinach, and almond milk.
2. Transfer to a bowl and sprinkle chia seeds on top.

15. Turkey and Cheese Roll-Ups

Total Time: 10 minutes

Serves: 2

Ingredients:

- 6 slices turkey

- 4 slices cheese
- 1/2 avocado, sliced
- Mustard for dipping

Instructions:

1. Arrange slices of turkey and top with avocado and cheese.
2. Roll, then use toothpicks to secure.
3. Accompany with mustard for a dip.

16. Green Keto Smoothie

Total Time: 5 minutes

Serves: 1

Ingredients:

- 1 cup unsweetened coconut milk
- 1/2 avocado
- Handful of spinach
- 1/4 cucumber
- 1/2 lemon, juiced
- Ice cubes (optional)

Instructions:

1. Smoothly blend avocado, spinach, cucumber, coconut milk, and lemon juice.
2. If desired, add some ice cubes.

17. Low-Carb Bagel with Cream Cheese and Smoked Salmon

Total Time: 10 minutes

Serves: 1

Ingredients:

- 1 low-carb bagel
- 2 tbsp cream cheese
- 2 oz smoked salmon
- Capers and dill for garnish

Instructions:

1. Toasted low-carb bagel.
2. Drizzle cream cheese over the bagel and place smoked salmon on top.
3. Add dill and capers as garnish.

18. Almond Flour Waffles

Total Time: 20 minutes

Cooking Time: 15 minutes

Serves: 2

Ingredients:

- 1 cup almond flour
- 2 eggs
- 1/2 cup unsweetened almond milk
- 1 tsp baking powder

- Vanilla extract to taste

Instructions:

1. Blend together almond flour, eggs, almond milk, vanilla extract, and baking powder.

2. Cook until golden brown in a waffle iron.

19. Baked Avocado Eggs

Total Time: 20 minutes

Cooking Time: 15 minutes

Serves: 2

Ingredients:

- 2 avocados
- 4 eggs
- Salt and pepper to taste
- Chopped parsley for garnish

Instructions:

1. Halve the avocados and remove the pits.

2. To provide space for the eggs, remove some meat.

3. After seasoning and cracking one egg into each half of an avocado, bake the eggs until set.

4. Add chopped parsley as a garnish.

20. Coconut Flour Porridge

Total Time: 15 minutes

Serves: 2

Ingredients:

- 1/2 cup coconut flour
- 2 cups unsweetened coconut milk
- 1 tsp vanilla extract
- Stevia or erythritol to taste
- Berries for topping

Instructions:

1. In a pot, combine sugar, vanilla extract, coconut flour, and coconut milk.
2. Stir over heat until thickened.
3. Drizzle with berries to serve.

21. Spinach and Feta Crustless Quiche

Total Time: 35 minutes

Cooking Time: 25 minutes

Serves: 4

Ingredients:

- 4 cups fresh spinach, chopped
- 1/2 cup feta cheese, crumbled
- 6 eggs
- 1 cup unsweetened almond milk
- Salt and pepper to taste

Instructions:

1. Turn the oven on to 375°F, or 190°C.

2. Add the spinach to a greased pie dish and sauté until it wilts.

3. Over the spinach, scatter the feta cheese.

4. Pour over spinach and feta after whisking together eggs, almond milk, salt, and pepper.

5. Bake the quiche until it sets and turns golden brown.

22. Keto Sausage and Egg Breakfast Casserole

Total Time: 45 minutes

Cooking Time: 30 minutes

Serves: 6

Ingredients:

- 1 lb breakfast sausage

- 8 eggs

- 1/2 cup heavy cream

- 1 cup shredded cheddar cheese

- Salt and pepper to taste

- Chopped green onions for garnish

Instructions:

1. After browning the sausage in a skillet, transfer it to a baking dish that has been oiled.

2. Combine cream, eggs, salt, and pepper in a bowl; transfer to the sausage.

3. Once the eggs are set, top with cheddar cheese and bake.

4. Add chopped green onions as a garnish.

23. Keto Blueberry Muffins

Total Time: 25 minutes

Cooking Time: 15 minutes

Serves: 6

Ingredients:

- 2 cups almond flour
- 1/4 cup melted butter
- 1/4 cup unsweetened almond milk
- 3 eggs
- 1/4 cup erythritol
- 1 tsp baking powder
- 1/2 cup fresh blueberries

Instructions:

1. Set oven temperature to 175°C/350°F.
2. Combine almond milk, eggs, erythritol, baking powder, melted butter, and almond flour.
3. Fold in blueberries gently.
4. Fill muffin cups with batter, then bake until golden.

24. Bacon and Egg Breakfast Salad

Total Time: 20 minutes

Cooking Time: 10 minutes

Serves: 2

Ingredients:

- 4 slices bacon
- 4 poached eggs
- Mixed salad greens
- Cherry tomatoes
- Avocado slices
- Balsamic vinaigrette

Instructions:

1. Crumble bacon when it's crispy.
2. Arrange avocado, cherry tomatoes, and salad leaves on plates.
3. Add some crumbled bacon and poached eggs on top.
4. Pour balsamic vinaigrette over.

25. Keto Coffee Smoothie

Total Time: 10 minutes

Serves: 1

Ingredients:

- 1 cup brewed coffee, chilled
- 1/4 cup unsweetened almond milk
- 1 tbsp MCT oil
- 1 scoop collagen powder
- Ice cubes

Instructions:

1. Smoothly blend ice cubes, cold coffee, almond milk, MCT oil, and collagen powder.

26. Low-Carb Breakfast Pizza

Total Time: 30 minutes

Cooking Time: 20 minutes

Serves: 2

Ingredients:

- 2 large portobello mushrooms, stems removed
- 1/2 cup pizza sauce (low-carb)
- 1/2 cup shredded mozzarella cheese
- 4 cherry tomatoes, sliced
- 2 slices cooked bacon, crumbled
- Fresh basil for garnish

Instructions:

1. Turn the oven on to 375°F, or 190°C.
2. Arrange the mushrooms on a baking sheet and top with bacon, cheese, tomatoes, and pizza sauce.
3. Bake the cheese until it's bubbling and melted.
4. Add some fresh basil as a garnish before serving.

27. Keto Peanut Butter Chia Pudding

Total Time: 5 minutes (plus chilling time)

Serves: 2

Ingredients:

- 1/4 cup chia seeds
- 1 cup unsweetened almond milk
- 2 tbsp peanut butter
- Stevia or erythritol to taste
- Crushed peanuts for topping

Instructions:

1. In a bowl, combine chia seeds, sugar, almond milk, and peanut butter.
2. Put it in the fridge to get thicker.
3. Before serving, sprinkle crushed peanuts on top.

28. Savory Keto Breakfast Muffins

Total Time: 30 minutes

Cooking Time: 20 minutes

Serves: 6

Ingredients:

- 6 eggs
- 1/4 cup heavy cream
- 1/2 cup shredded cheddar cheese
- 1/4 cup diced bell peppers
- 1/4 cup diced onions
- 1/4 cup cooked and crumbled sausage

- Salt and pepper to taste

Instructions:

1. Set oven temperature to 175°C/350°F.

2. Beat together eggs, heavy cream, pepper, and salt.

3. Add the sausage, bell peppers, onions, and cheese and stir.

4. Fill muffin tins with oil, then bake until solidified.

29. Keto Almond Joy Chia Seed Pudding

Total Time: 5 minutes (plus overnight chilling)

Serves: 2

Ingredients:

- 1/4 cup chia seeds

- 1 cup unsweetened coconut milk

- 1 tbsp unsweetened cocoa powder

- 2 tbsp shredded coconut

- Stevia or erythritol to taste

- Almonds for topping

Instructions:

1. In a container, combine chia seeds, sweetener, shredded coconut, coconut milk, and cocoa powder.

2. Store in the fridge all night.

3. Serve with almonds sprinkled over top.

30. Keto Breakfast Stuffed Bell Peppers

Total Time: 40 minutes

Cooking Time: 30 minutes

Serves: 4

Ingredients:

- 2 bell peppers, halved and seeds removed
- 8 eggs
- 1/2 cup diced ham
- 1/4 cup diced tomatoes
- 1/4 cup shredded cheddar cheese
- Salt and pepper to taste
- Chopped parsley for garnish

Instructions:

1. Turn the oven on to 375°F, or 190°C.
2. Arrange the halves of bell peppers on a baking sheet.
3. After cracking an egg into each pepper half, garnish with cheese, ham, and tomatoes.
4. Eggs should be baked until set.
5. Before serving, garnish with chopped parsley.

31. Keto Egg and Cheese Breakfast Wrap

Total Time: 15 minutes

Cooking Time: 10 minutes

Serves: 1

Ingredients:

- 2 large eggs

- 1/4 cup shredded cheddar cheese

- 1 tbsp butter

- Salt and pepper to taste

- Low-carb tortilla

Instructions:

1. Add butter to a pan and scramble the eggs.

2. Over the eggs, scatter the shredded cheddar cheese.

3. Add salt and pepper for seasoning, then transfer onto a low-carb tortilla and wrap.

32. Keto Cauliflower Breakfast Hash

Total Time: 25 minutes

Cooking Time: 20 minutes

Serves: 4

Ingredients:

- 1 medium cauliflower, grated

- 4 slices bacon, chopped

- 1/2 cup diced bell peppers

- 1/4 cup diced onions

- 4 eggs

- Salt and pepper to taste

Instructions:

1. After the bacon is crispy, add the onions and bell peppers to a skillet.

2. Cook the grated cauliflower until it becomes soft.

3. In the cauliflower mixture, create wells and crack eggs into them.

4. Cook the eggs covered until they reach your desired doneness.

33. Keto Avocado and Bacon Egg Cups

Total Time: 20 minutes

Cooking Time: 15 minutes

Serves: 2

Ingredients:

- 2 avocados, halved and pitted
- 4 eggs
- 4 slices bacon, cooked and crumbled
- Chives for garnish
- Salt and pepper to taste

Instructions:

1. Turn the oven on to 375°F, or 190°C.

2. Remove a tiny amount of avocado from each half using a spoon.

3. Arrange the avocados on a baking sheet and split each one in half.

4. Add salt, pepper, and bacon crumbles on top.

5. Bake the eggs until they are set.

6. Sprinkle chopped chives over top.

34. Keto Zucchini and Bacon Fritters

Total Time: 25 minutes

Cooking Time: 15 minutes

Serves: 3

Ingredients:

- 2 medium zucchinis, grated
- 4 slices bacon, cooked and crumbled
- 2 eggs
- 1/4 cup almond flour
- 1/4 cup grated Parmesan cheese
- Salt and pepper to taste

Instructions:

1. Mix together the grated zucchini, bacon, eggs, Parmesan, almond flour, salt, and pepper.
2. Dollop the ingredients onto a heated pan that has been lightly oiled.
3. Cook until both sides are golden brown.

35. Keto Cheddar and Broccoli Egg Muffins

Total Time: 30 minutes

Cooking Time: 20 minutes

Serves: 4

Ingredients:

- 6 eggs
- 1/2 cup shredded cheddar cheese

- 1 cup steamed broccoli, chopped
- 1/4 cup heavy cream
- Salt and pepper to taste

Instructions:

1. Set the oven's temperature to 175°C/350°F.

2. Beat eggs and add broccoli, cheddar cheese, heavy cream, salt, and pepper.

3. Fill muffin tins with mixture after greasing them.

4. Bake until the egg muffins are set.

36. Keto Pumpkin Spice Pancakes

Total Time: 20 minutes

Cooking Time: 15 minutes

Serves: 2

Ingredients:

- 1/2 cup almond flour
- 2 eggs
- 1/4 cup pumpkin puree
- 1 tsp pumpkin spice
- 1/4 tsp baking powder
- Butter for cooking

Instructions:

1. Combine almond flour, eggs, baking powder, pumpkin puree, and pumpkin spice.

2. Melt butter in a pan, then ladle batter onto it.

3. Stir and continue cooking until bubbles appear on one side of the food.

37. Keto Ham and Cheese Breakfast Casserole

Total Time: 40 minutes

Cooking Time: 30 minutes

Serves: 6

Ingredients:

- 1 lb cooked ham, diced

- 8 eggs

- 1/2 cup heavy cream

- 1 cup shredded cheddar cheese

- 1/2 cup diced bell peppers

- Salt and pepper to taste

Instructions:

1. Turn the oven on to 375°F, or 190°C.

2. Combine eggs, cheddar cheese, ham, heavy cream, bell peppers, and salt & pepper.

3. Spoon onto a baking dish that has been buttered, then bake until firm and caramelized.

38. Keto Cinnamon Almond Butter Smoothie

Total Time: 10 minutes

Serves: 1

Ingredients:

- 1 cup unsweetened almond milk
- 2 tbsp almond butter
- 1/2 tsp cinnamon
- 1 scoop vanilla protein powder
- Ice cubes

Instructions:

1. Smoothly blend ice cubes, protein powder, cinnamon, almond butter, and almond milk.

39. Keto Egg and Bacon Breakfast Tacos

Total Time: 20 minutes

Cooking Time: 15 minutes

Serves: 2

Ingredients:

- 4 eggs
- 4 slices bacon, cooked and crumbled
- 4 low-carb tortillas
- 1/2 cup shredded cheddar cheese
- Avocado slices for topping

Instructions:

1. Add crumbled bacon to scrambled eggs.
2. Spoon mixture into tortillas low in carbohydrates.
3. Add avocado slices and shredded cheddar cheese on top.

40. Keto Coconut Flour Porridge with Berries

Total Time: 15 minutes

Serves: 2

Ingredients:

- 1/2 cup coconut flour
- 2 cups unsweetened almond milk
- 1 tsp vanilla extract
- Stevia or erythritol to taste
- Mixed berries for topping

Instructions:

1. In a pot, combine sugar, vanilla extract, almond milk, and coconut flour.
2. Stir over heat until thickened.
3. Before serving, sprinkle mixed berries on top.

41. Keto Cheddar and Jalapeño Egg Bites

Total Time: 25 minutes

Cooking Time: 15 minutes

Serves: 4

Ingredients:

- 6 eggs
- 1/2 cup shredded cheddar cheese
- 1/4 cup diced jalapeños

- 1/4 cup heavy cream
- Salt and pepper to taste

Instructions:

1. Set the oven's temperature to 175°C/350°F.

2. Beat eggs, then stir in heavy cream, cheddar cheese, jalapeños, salt, and pepper.

3. Fill small muffin cups with grease. Pour mixture into cups.

4. Preheat the oven to a mild golden color and set the egg bits.

42. Keto Cinnamon Roll Mug Cake

Total Time: 10 minutes

Serves: 1

Ingredients:

- 3 tbsp almond flour
- 1 tbsp butter, melted
- 1 tbsp cream cheese, softened
- 1 egg
- 1/2 tsp baking powder
- 1/2 tsp cinnamon
- 1 tbsp erythritol

Instructions:

1. In a mug, stir together almond flour, cream cheese, melted butter, egg, baking powder, cinnamon, and erythritol.

2. Once the cake is firm, microwave it for two to three minutes.

43. Keto Smoked Salmon and Cream Cheese Roll-Ups

Total Time: 10 minutes

Serves: 2

Ingredients:

- 4 oz smoked salmon
- 4 tbsp cream cheese
- 1 tbsp capers
- Fresh dill for garnish

Instructions:

1. Arrange the slices of smoked salmon.
2. Top each slice with a layer of cream cheese and garnish with capers.
3. Garnish with fresh dill and roll up.

44. Keto Almond Flour Waffles with Berries

Total Time: 20 minutes

Cooking Time: 15 minutes

Serves: 2

Ingredients:

- 1 cup almond flour
- 2 eggs
- 1/2 cup unsweetened almond milk
- 1 tsp baking powder
- 1 tsp vanilla extract

- Mixed berries for topping

Instructions:

1. Blend together almond flour, eggs, almond milk, vanilla extract, and baking powder.

2. Cook until golden brown in a waffle iron.

3. Before serving, sprinkle mixed berries on top.

45. Keto Chia Seed and Berry Parfait
Total Time: 10 minutes (plus chilling time)

Serves: 2

Ingredients:

- 1/4 cup chia seeds

- 1 cup unsweetened coconut milk

- Stevia or erythritol to taste

- 1/2 cup mixed berries

- 2 tbsp unsweetened shredded coconut

Instructions:

1. In a bowl, combine sugar, coconut milk, and chia seeds.

2. Put it in the fridge to get thicker.

3. Arrange shredded coconut and mixed berries on top of the chia pudding.

46. Keto Broccoli and Cheese Egg Muffins
Total Time: 30 minutes

Cooking Time: 20 minutes

Serves: 4

Ingredients:

- 6 eggs

- 1 cup cooked broccoli, chopped

- 1/2 cup shredded cheddar cheese

- 1/4 cup heavy cream

- Salt and pepper to taste

Instructions:

1. Set the oven's temperature to 175°C/350°F.

2. Beat eggs and add cooked broccoli, heavy cream, cheddar cheese, salt, and pepper.

3. Fill muffin tins with mixture after greasing them.

4. Bake the muffins until the eggs are set.

47. Keto Blueberry and Almond Flour Muffins
Total Time: 25 minutes

Cooking Time: 15 minutes

Serves: 6

Ingredients:

- 1 cup almond flour

- 2 eggs

- 1/4 cup melted coconut oil

- 1/4 cup unsweetened almond milk

- 1/4 cup erythritol
- 1 tsp baking powder
- 1/2 cup fresh blueberries

Instructions:

1. Set oven temperature to 175°C/350°F.
2. Combine almond milk, erythritol, eggs, melted coconut oil, and baking powder.
3. Fold in blueberries gently.
4. Fill muffin cups with batter, then bake until golden.

48. Keto Breakfast Cobb Salad

Total Time: 15 minutes

Serves: 2

Ingredients:

- 4 slices bacon, cooked and crumbled
- 4 boiled eggs, sliced
- 1 avocado, diced
- 1 cup cherry tomatoes, halved
- 1/2 cup crumbled feta cheese
- Salt and pepper to taste
- Ranch dressing for topping

Instructions:

1. In a bowl, arrange the bacon, boiled eggs, avocado, tomatoes, and feta.

2. Add pepper and salt for seasoning.

3. Before serving, drizzle with ranch dressing.

49. Keto Peanut Butter and Jelly Chia Pudding

Total Time: 5 minutes (plus chilling time)

Serves: 2

Ingredients:

- 1/4 cup chia seeds
- 1 cup unsweetened almond milk
- 2 tbsp peanut butter
- Sugar-free jelly or jam
- Crushed peanuts for topping

Instructions:

1. In a jar, combine almond milk, peanut butter, and chia seeds.

2. Put it in the fridge to get thicker.

3. Before serving, swirl with sugar-free jelly or jam and sprinkle crushed peanuts on top.

50. Keto Breakfast BLT Salad

Total Time: 20 minutes

Serves: 2

Ingredients:

- 4 cups mixed salad greens
- 8 slices bacon, cooked and crumbled

- 2 boiled eggs, sliced
- 1 cup cherry tomatoes, halved
- Avocado slices
- Ranch dressing for topping

Instructions:

1. Combine cherry tomatoes, bacon, boiled eggs, and salad greens in a bowl.
2. Add slices of avocado on top.
3. Before serving, drizzle with ranch dressing.

Launch Recipes

1. Grilled Chicken Caesar Salad

Total Time: 30 minutes

Cooking Time: 15 minutes

Serves: 2

Ingredients:

- 2 boneless, skinless chicken breasts
- Romaine lettuce, chopped
- Cherry tomatoes, halved
- Parmesan cheese, grated
- Caesar dressing (low-carb)

Instructions:

1. Add salt and pepper to chicken breasts for seasoning.

2. Cook the chicken on the grill until it's done.

3. Grilled chicken should be cut into strips.

4. Combine the lettuce, tomatoes, grilled chicken, and Parmesan in a big bowl.

5. After serving, drizzle with Caesar dressing.

2. Zucchini Noodles with Pesto and Cherry Tomatoes

Total Time: 20 minutes

Cooking Time: 10 minutes

Serves: 2

Ingredients:

- 2 large zucchinis, spiralized

- Pesto sauce (low-carb)

- Cherry tomatoes, halved

- Pine nuts (optional)

Instructions:

1. Zest the zucchini into spirals to make noodles.

2. Sauté zucchini noodles in a pan until they become soft.

3. Toss with cherry tomatoes and pesto sauce.

4. Prior to serving, you might choose to garnish with pine nuts.

3. Turkey and Avocado Lettuce Wraps

Total Time: 15 minutes

Cooking Time: 10 minutes

Serves: 4

Ingredients:

- 1 lb ground turkey
- Lettuce leaves (e.g., iceberg or butter lettuce)
- Avocado, sliced
- Salsa (low-carb)

Instructions:

1. Brown ground turkey after cooking.
2. Place turkey onto a bed of lettuce.
3. Add salsa and avocado slices on top.
4. Enjoy after wrapping!

4. Cauliflower Fried Rice with Shrimp

Total Time: 25 minutes

Cooking Time: 15 minutes

Serves: 4

Ingredients:

- 1 cauliflower, grated
- Shrimp, peeled and deveined
- Mixed vegetables (e.g., peas, carrots, and bell peppers)
- Soy sauce (low-carb)

Instructions:

1. Crush cauliflower to a rice-like texture.

2. In a pan, sauté the shrimp and veggies.

3. Cook the cauliflower rice until it becomes soft.

4. Use low-carb soy sauce for seasoning.

5. Egg Salad Lettuce Wraps

Total Time: 15 minutes

Cooking Time: 10 minutes

Serves: 2

Ingredients:

- Hard-boiled eggs, chopped

- Mayonnaise (low-carb)

- Dijon mustard

- Lettuce leaves

Instructions:

1. Combine chopped eggs with Dijon mustard and mayonnaise.

2. Place egg salad onto leaves of lettuce.

3. After wrapping, serve.

6. Caprese Salad Skewers

Total Time: 15 minutes

Cooking Time: 0 minutes

Serves: 4

Ingredients:

- Cherry tomatoes
- Fresh mozzarella balls
- Basil leaves
- Balsamic glaze (low-carb)

Instructions:

1. Put mozzarella, basil, and tomatoes on skewers.

2. Before serving, drizzle with balsamic glaze.

7. Salmon and Avocado Salad

Total Time: 20 minutes

Cooking Time: 15 minutes

Serves: 2

Ingredients:

- Salmon fillets
- Mixed salad greens
- Avocado, sliced
- Lemon vinaigrette (low-carb)

Instructions:

1. Bake or grill fish until it's done.

2. Place the mixed greens in a platter.

3. Place slices of avocado and salmon on top.

4. Pour a lemon vinaigrette over it.

8. Broccoli and Cheddar Stuffed Chicken

Total Time: 40 minutes

Cooking Time: 25 minutes

Serves: 4

Ingredients:

- 4 boneless, skinless chicken breasts
- Broccoli florets, steamed
- Cheddar cheese, shredded
- Garlic powder, salt, and pepper

Instructions:

1. Turn the oven on to 375°F, or 190°C.
2. On each of the chicken breasts, cut a pocket.
3. Stuff with cheddar and cooked broccoli.
4. Add pepper, salt, and garlic powder for seasoning.
5. Bake the chicken until it's thoroughly done.

9. Shrimp and Avocado Ceviche

Total Time: 20 minutes

Cooking Time: 0 minutes (if using pre-cooked shrimp)

Serves: 4

Ingredients:

- Cooked shrimp, chopped
- Avocado, diced
- Red onion, finely chopped

- Cilantro, chopped
- Lime juice

Instructions:

1. Add the shrimp, avocado, cilantro, and onion.
2. Add some freshly squeezed lime juice to the mixture.
3. Before serving, chill.

10. Greek Salad with Grilled Lamb

Total Time: 30 minutes

Cooking Time: 15 minutes

Serves: 4

Ingredients:

- Lamb chops
- Cucumber, diced
- Kalamata olives, sliced
- Feta cheese, crumbled
- Greek dressing (low-carb)

Instructions:

1. Once done, grill the lamb chops.
2. In a bowl, mix the cucumber, feta, and olives.
3. Place the cooked lamb there.
4. Pour on some Greek dressing.

11. Cauliflower Crust Pizza

Total Time: 40 minutes

Cooking Time: 25 minutes

Serves: 4

Ingredients:

- Cauliflower, grated
- Eggs
- Mozzarella cheese, shredded
- Low-carb pizza sauce
- Toppings of your choice (e.g., pepperoni, olives, mushrooms)

Instructions:

1. To make a dough, combine eggs, mozzarella, and grated cauliflower.
2. To make a crust, press the dough onto a baking sheet.
3. Bake till the color turns golden.
4. Apply pizza sauce, top with ingredients, and bake until the cheese is melted.

12. Spinach and Feta Stuffed Chicken Breast

Total Time: 35 minutes

Cooking Time: 20 minutes

Serves: 2

Ingredients:

- Chicken breasts
- Fresh spinach, chopped

- Feta cheese, crumbled
- Garlic, minced
- Olive oil

Instructions:

1. Turn the oven on to 400°F, or 200°C.

2. Combine garlic, feta, and spinach.

3. Make indentations on each chicken breast, then fill them with the mixture.

4. Bake the chicken until it's thoroughly done.

13. Turkey and Vegetable Skewers

Total Time: 30 minutes

Cooking Time: 15 minutes

Serves: 4

Ingredients:

- Turkey breast, cubed
- Bell peppers, sliced
- Red onion, diced
- Zucchini, sliced
- Olive oil
- Italian seasoning

Instructions:

1. Skewers with veggies and turkey should be threaded.

2. Apply a thin layer of olive oil and season to taste.

3. Cook the turkey and vegetables on the grill until they are soft.

14. Mushroom and Swiss Turkey Burger

Total Time: 25 minutes

Cooking Time: 15 minutes

Serves: 2

Ingredients:

- Ground turkey
- Mushrooms, sliced
- Swiss cheese slices
- Lettuce leaves
- Tomato slices

Instructions:

1. Patties out of the turkey should be grilled.
2. Sauté the mushrooms until they become soft.
3. Top burgers with sautéed mushrooms and Swiss cheese.
4. Arrange tomato slices on lettuce "buns" and serve.

15. Eggplant Lasagna

Total Time: 50 minutes

Cooking Time: 30 minutes

Serves: 6

Ingredients:

- Eggplant, thinly sliced

- Ground beef or turkey
- Low-carb marinara sauce
- Ricotta cheese
- Mozzarella cheese, shredded

Instructions:

1. Bake or grill slices of eggplant until they are soft.

2. Gravy is ground, then combined with marinara.

3. Arrange the eggplant, mozzarella, ricotta, and meat sauce in a baking dish.

4. Bake till frothy.

16. Cabbage and Sausage Stir-Fry

Total Time: 25 minutes

Cooking Time: 15 minutes

Serves: 4

Ingredients:

- Cabbage, shredded
- Sausage links, sliced
- Bell peppers, sliced
- Soy sauce (low-carb)
- Sesame oil

Instructions:

1. Brown sausage through sautéing.

2. Stir-fry the bell peppers and cabbage until the vegetables are soft.

3. Use sesame oil and low-carb soy sauce for seasoning.

17. Shrimp and Broccoli Alfredo

Total Time: 30 minutes

Cooking Time: 20 minutes

Serves: 4

Ingredients:

- Shrimp, peeled and deveined
- Broccoli florets
- Heavy cream
- Parmesan cheese, grated
- Garlic powder

Instructions:

1. Shrimp should be pan-fried till pink.
2. Broccoli should be steamed until soft.
3. To make Alfredo sauce, combine heavy cream, Parmesan, and garlic powder.
4. Stir together broccoli, shrimp, and sauce.

18. Avocado Tuna Salad

Total Time: 15 minutes

Cooking Time: 0 minutes

Serves: 2

Ingredients:

- Canned tuna, drained

- Avocado, mashed

- Red onion, finely chopped

- Celery, diced

- Lemon juice

Instructions:

1. Mix tuna, celery, red onion, and mashed avocado.

2. Add some freshly squeezed lemon juice to the mixture.

3. Serve in a low-carb wrap or on lettuce leaves.

19. Sesame Ginger Chicken Salad

Total Time: 30 minutes

Cooking Time: 20 minutes

Serves: 2

Ingredients:

- Chicken breast, grilled and sliced

- Mixed salad greens

- Cucumber, julienned

- Sesame seeds

- Ginger dressing (low-carb)

Instructions:

1. After the chicken is cooked, slice it.

2. Toss cucumber and salad greens.

3. Add sesame seeds, chopped chicken, and ginger dressing on top.

20. Cajun Shrimp Lettuce Wraps

Total Time: 20 minutes

Cooking Time: 10 minutes

Serves: 2

Ingredients:

- Cajun seasoning
- Shrimp, peeled and deveined
- Avocado, sliced
- Cherry tomatoes, halved
- Lettuce leaves

Instructions:

1. Add Cajun spice to the shrimp and simmer until they become pink.

2. Put shrimp, avocado, and tomatoes on lettuce wraps.

21. Mediterranean Chicken Skewers

Total Time: 30 minutes

Cooking Time: 15 minutes

Serves: 4

Ingredients:

- Chicken breast, cut into chunks
- Cherry tomatoes
- Red onion, sliced

- Zucchini, sliced
- Olive oil
- Lemon juice
- Oregano, dried

Instructions:

1. Put veggies and chicken on skewers.
2. Drizzle with lemon juice, olive oil, and oregano.
3. Cook the chicken on the grill until it's done.

22. Cabbage Roll Bowls

Total Time: 40 minutes

Cooking Time: 25 minutes

Serves: 4

Ingredients:

- Ground beef
- Cabbage, shredded
- Cauliflower rice
- Tomato sauce (low-carb)
- Italian seasoning

Instructions:

1. In a pan, brown the ground meat.
2. Add the cauliflower rice and the shredded cabbage.
3. Add Italian spice and tomato sauce and stir.

4. Simmer the cabbage until it becomes soft.

23. Shirataki Noodle Stir-Fry

Total Time: 25 minutes

Cooking Time: 15 minutes

Serves: 2

Ingredients:

- Shirataki noodles

- Chicken or tofu, diced

- Broccoli florets

- Soy sauce (low-carb)

- Ginger, grated

- Garlic, minced

Instructions:

1. After rinsing, set aside the shirataki noodles.

2. Add the garlic, ginger, broccoli, and chicken or tofu and sauté.

3. Add the soy sauce and shirataki noodles.

4. Stir-fry until well hot.

24. Greek Turkey Burgers

Total Time: 30 minutes

Cooking Time: 20 minutes

Serves: 4

Ingredients:

- Ground turkey

- Feta cheese, crumbled

- Black olives, chopped

- Spinach, chopped

- Tzatziki sauce (low-carb)

Instructions:

1. Combine spinach, feta, olives, and ground turkey.

2. After shaping into patties, grill.

3. Top with a generous portion of tzatziki sauce.

25. Cajun Chicken Lettuce Wraps

Total Time: 25 minutes

Cooking Time: 15 minutes

Serves: 2

Ingredients:

- Chicken thighs, seasoned with Cajun spices

- Bell peppers, sliced

- Avocado, sliced

- Lettuce leaves

Instructions:

1. Cook or grill the chicken until it's done.

2. Peppers should be sautéed till soft.

3. Combine the avocado, peppers, and chicken to make lettuce wraps.

26. Salmon and Asparagus Foil Packets

Total Time: 30 minutes

Cooking Time: 20 minutes

Serves: 2

Ingredients:

- Salmon fillets
- Asparagus spears
- Lemon slices
- Dill, chopped
- Olive oil

Instructions:

1. Arrange the asparagus and fish on foil.
2. Add lemon slices, drizzle with olive oil, and top with dill.
3. Once the salmon is cooked, bake the sealed packets.

27. Broccoli and Bacon Egg Muffins

Total Time: 30 minutes

Cooking Time: 20 minutes

Serves: 6

Ingredients:

- Eggs
- Broccoli, chopped
- Bacon, cooked and crumbled

- Cheddar cheese, shredded

Instructions:

1. In a bowl, whisk the eggs.

2. Add cheese, bacon, and broccoli and stir.

3. Fill muffin tins, then bake for firmness.

28. Mexican Cauliflower Rice Bowl

Total Time: 25 minutes

Cooking Time: 15 minutes

Serves: 2

Ingredients:

- Cauliflower rice

- Ground beef or turkey

- Taco seasoning (low-carb)

- Avocado, diced

- Salsa

Instructions:

1. Saute ground beef while adding taco spice.

2. Cook rice made from cauliflower until soft.

3. Put meat, avocado, salsa, and cauliflower rice in dishes.

29. Lemon Herb Grilled Shrimp

Total Time: 20 minutes

Cooking Time: 10 minutes

Serves: 4

Ingredients:

- Shrimp, peeled and deveined
- Lemon zest and juice
- Fresh herbs (e.g., parsley, thyme)
- Olive oil

Instructions:

1. Toss shrimp with olive oil, lemon juice, zest, and herbs.
2. Grill the prawns until they turn opaque.

30. Tofu and Vegetable Stir-Fry

Total Time: 30 minutes

Cooking Time: 20 minutes

Serves: 3

Ingredients:

- Firm tofu, cubed
- Broccoli florets
- Bell peppers, sliced
- Snow peas
- Low-carb stir-fry sauce

Instructions:

1. Tofu is sautéed till golden.
2. When the veggies are soft, add them and stir-fry.

3. Stir-fry sauce should be added and mixed in.

31. Cajun Cauliflower Bites

Total Time: 25 minutes

Cooking Time: 15 minutes

Serves: 4

Ingredients:

- Cauliflower florets
- Cajun seasoning
- Almond flour
- Eggs
- Olive oil

Instructions:

1. Vegetable florets are dipped in beaten eggs.
2. Apply a coating made of almond flour and Cajun spice.
3. Bake till crisp and golden.

32. Turkey and Avocado Lettuce Cups

Total Time: 15 minutes

Cooking Time: 10 minutes

Serves: 2

Ingredients:

- Ground turkey
- Taco seasoning (low-carb)

- Lettuce leaves

- Avocado, sliced

- Salsa

Instructions:

1. Add taco seasoning to ground turkey and cook.

2. Transfer to lettuce cups using a spoon.

3. Add salsa and sliced avocado on top.

33. Italian Zoodle Salad

Total Time: 20 minutes

Cooking Time: 10 minutes

Serves: 2

Ingredients:

- Zucchini noodles (zoodles)

- Cherry tomatoes, halved

- Mozzarella balls

- Fresh basil leaves

- Olive oil and balsamic vinegar

Instructions:

1. Zoodles should be sautéed till soft.

2. Add basil, mozzarella, and tomatoes and toss.

3. Drizzle with balsamic vinegar and olive oil.

34. Spaghetti Squash with Pesto and Chicken

Total Time: 45 minutes

Cooking Time: 30 minutes

Serves: 4

Ingredients:

- Spaghetti squash, roasted and shredded

- Grilled chicken breast, sliced

- Pesto sauce (low-carb)

- Cherry tomatoes, halved

- Parmesan cheese, grated

Instructions:

1. Shred spaghetti squash using a fork after roasting it.

2. Toss with tomatoes, Parmesan, pesto, and grilled chicken.

35. Stuffed Bell Peppers with Ground Beef

Total Time: 45 minutes

Cooking Time: 30 minutes

Serves: 4

Ingredients:

- Bell peppers, halved

- Ground beef

- Cauliflower rice

- Tomato sauce (low-carb)

- Italian herbs

Instructions:

1. Combine brown ground beef, seasonings, and cauliflower rice.

2. Bake bell peppers filled with stuffing until they are soft.

36. Asian-Inspired Salmon Lettuce Wraps

Total Time: 25 minutes

Cooking Time: 15 minutes

Serves: 2

Ingredients:

- Salmon fillets, grilled and flaked

- Bibb lettuce leaves

- Shredded carrots

- Cucumber, julienned

- Hoisin sauce (low-carb)

Instructions:

1. Flake salmon after grilling it.

2. Combine cucumber, carrots, salmon, and lettuce to make wraps.

3. Pour some low-carb hoisin sauce over top.

37. Egg Drop Soup with Shrimp

Total Time: 20 minutes

Cooking Time: 15 minutes

Serves: 4

Ingredients:

- Shrimp, peeled and deveined
- Chicken broth
- Eggs, beaten
- Green onions, sliced
- Soy sauce (low-carb)

Instructions:

1. Simmer chicken broth for a while.

2. Cook the prawns until they turn pink.

3. Stirring constantly, gradually add in the beaten eggs.

4. Add soy sauce for seasoning and green onions for garnish.

38. Mexican Chicken Cauliflower Rice Bowl

Total Time: 30 minutes

Cooking Time: 20 minutes

Serves: 2

Ingredients:

- Cauliflower rice
- Grilled chicken, sliced
- Black beans (optional)
- Avocado, diced
- Salsa

Instructions:

1. Cook rice made from cauliflower until soft.

2. Put chicken, black beans, avocado, and salsa in bowls.

39. Broccoli and Cheddar Soup

Total Time: 30 minutes

Cooking Time: 20 minutes

Serves: 4

Ingredients:

- Broccoli florets
- Chicken or vegetable broth
- Heavy cream
- Cheddar cheese, shredded
- Salt and pepper

Instructions:

1. After steaming, puree the broccoli with the broth.
2. Put cheese and heavy cream back on the stove.
3. Add pepper and salt for seasoning.

40. Mushroom and Spinach Omelette

Total Time: 15 minutes

Cooking Time: 10 minutes

Serves: 2

Ingredients:

- Eggs
- Mushrooms, sliced

- Spinach leaves
- Feta cheese, crumbled
- Olive oil

Instructions:

1. In olive oil, sauté spinach and mushrooms.
2. Beat eggs and pour onto vegetables.
3. When the eggs are set, mix in the feta and simmer.

41. Salmon and Avocado Stuffed Bell Peppers

Total Time: 30 minutes

Cooking Time: 20 minutes

Serves: 4

Ingredients:

- Bell peppers, halved
- Canned salmon, drained
- Avocado, mashed
- Red onion, finely chopped
- Dill, chopped

Instructions:

1. Combine salmon, dill, red onion, and mashed avocado.
2. Stuff mixture into bell peppers.
3. Bake peppers until they become soft.

42. Cauliflower and Ham Casserole

Total Time: 45 minutes

Cooking Time: 30 minutes

Serves: 6

Ingredients:

- Cauliflower florets, steamed
- Cooked ham, diced
- Heavy cream
- Cheddar cheese, shredded
- Mustard (low-carb)

Instructions:

1. Combine the mustard, cream, ham, and cauliflower.
2. Place in a baking dish, sprinkle cheese on top, and bake for bubbling.

43. Lemon Garlic Shrimp Salad

Total Time: 20 minutes

Cooking Time: 10 minutes

Serves: 2

Ingredients:

- Shrimp, peeled and deveined
- Mixed salad greens
- Cherry tomatoes, halved
- Lemon juice
- Garlic, minced

- Olive oil

Instructions:

1. Sauté garlic and shrimp till pink.

2. Toss tomatoes and salad greens.

3. Add cooked shrimp on top, then drizzle with olive oil and lemon juice.

44. Cabbage and Sausage Skillet

Total Time: 30 minutes

Cooking Time: 20 minutes

Serves: 4

Ingredients:

- Sausage links, sliced

- Cabbage, shredded

- Onion, sliced

- Garlic powder

- Paprika

Instructions:

1. Sausage is browned on a skillet.

2. Add the paprika, garlic powder, onion, and cabbage.

3. Cook cabbage until it becomes soft.

45. Caprese Stuffed Portobello Mushrooms

Total Time: 25 minutes

Cooking Time: 15 minutes

Serves: 2

Ingredients:

- Portobello mushrooms, cleaned

- Mozzarella cheese, sliced

- Cherry tomatoes, sliced

- Fresh basil leaves

- Balsamic glaze (low-carb)

Instructions:

1. Arrange the mushrooms on a baking tray.

2. Add cheese, tomatoes, and basil on top.

3. Bake the mushrooms until they become soft.

4. Before serving, drizzle with balsamic glaze.

46. Turkey and Broccoli Alfredo Zoodles

Total Time: 30 minutes

Cooking Time: 20 minutes

Serves: 2

Ingredients:

- Zucchini noodles (zoodles)

- Ground turkey

- Broccoli florets

- Alfredo sauce (low-carb)

- Parmesan cheese, grated

Instructions:

1. Turkey minced and sautéed till browned.

2. Cook the broccoli until it becomes soft.

3. Add the Parmesan, Alfredo sauce, and zoodles.

47. Chicken Caesar Lettuce Wraps

Total Time: 20 minutes

Cooking Time: 10 minutes

Serves: 2

Ingredients:

- Cooked chicken breast, shredded

- Romaine lettuce leaves

- Caesar dressing (low-carb)

- Parmesan cheese, grated

Instructions:

1. Place shredded chicken within lettuce leaves.

2. Season with Parmesan and drizzle with Caesar dressing.

48. Sesame Ginger Tofu Stir-Fry

Total Time: 30 minutes

Cooking Time: 20 minutes

Serves: 3

Ingredients:

- Firm tofu, cubed

- Broccoli florets

- Bell peppers, sliced

- Soy sauce (low-carb)

- Sesame oil

- Ginger, grated

Instructions:

1. Tofu is sautéed till golden.

2. Stir-fry the bell peppers and broccoli until they are soft.

3. Stir in the grated ginger, sesame oil, and soy sauce.

49. Avocado and Shrimp Spring Rolls

Total Time: 25 minutes

Cooking Time: 10 minutes

Serves: 4

Ingredients:

- Rice paper wrappers

- Shrimp, cooked and peeled

- Avocado, sliced

- Cucumber, julienned

- Mint leaves

Instructions:

1. Dip wrappers made of rice paper in warm water.

2. Stuff with shrimp, cucumber, avocado, and mint.

3. Tightly roll and present.

50. Buffalo Chicken Lettuce Wraps

Total Time: 25 minutes

Cooking Time: 15 minutes

Serves: 2

Ingredients:

- Shredded cooked chicken

- Buffalo sauce (low-carb)

- Blue cheese crumbles

- Lettuce leaves

Instructions:

1. Combine buffalo sauce with the shredded chicken.

2. Spoon into the leaves of the lettuce.

3. Add crumbled blue cheese on top.

Dinner Recipes

1. Grilled Chicken Caesar Salad

Total Time: 30 minutes

Cooking Time: 15 minutes

Serves: 2

Ingredients:

- 2 boneless, skinless chicken breasts
- Romaine lettuce
- Parmesan cheese, grated
- Caesar dressing
- Olive oil
- Salt and pepper to taste

Instructions:

1. Set the grill's temperature to medium-high.
2. Chicken breasts should be seasoned with salt and pepper, brushed with olive oil, and cooked on the grill.
3. Romaine lettuce should be chopped and put in a bowl.
4. Add the sliced grilled chicken to the lettuce.
5. Drizzle with Caesar dressing and top with Parmesan cheese.
6. After gently tossing the salad, serve.

2. Zucchini Noodles with Pesto and Cherry Tomatoes

Total Time: 20 minutes

Cooking Time: 10 minutes

Serves: 2

Ingredients:

- 2 large zucchinis, spiralized
- 1 cup cherry tomatoes, halved
- 1/2 cup pesto sauce

- Olive oil

- Salt and pepper to taste

- Grated Parmesan cheese (optional)

Instructions:

1. In a pan set over medium heat, warm the olive oil.

2. When the cherry tomatoes begin to soften, add them and simmer.

3. When tender, add the zucchini noodles and sauté for 5 to 7 minutes.

4. Add the pesto sauce and season with the pepper and salt.

5. Optional: Before serving, sprinkle some grated Parmesan cheese on top.

3. Salmon with Lemon Dill Sauce

Total Time: 25 minutes

Cooking Time: 15 minutes

Serves: 2

Ingredients:

- 2 salmon fillets

- 2 tablespoons olive oil

- 1 lemon, juiced

- 2 tablespoons fresh dill, chopped

- Salt and pepper to taste

Instructions:

1. Set oven temperature to 400°F, or 200°C.

2. Salmon fillets should be put on a baking sheet, brushed with olive oil, and salted and peppered.

3. Bake the salmon for 15 minutes, or until it is thoroughly cooked.

4. Combine the lemon juice and chopped dill in a small bowl.

5. To serve, spoon the cooked salmon with the lemon-dill sauce.

4. Eggplant Lasagna

Total Time: 45 minutes

Cooking Time: 30 minutes

Serves: 4

Ingredients:

- 1 large eggplant, thinly sliced

- 1 pound ground beef

- 2 cups marinara sauce

- 2 cups ricotta cheese

- 1 cup mozzarella cheese, shredded

- 1/2 cup Parmesan cheese, grated

- Fresh basil for garnish

- Salt and pepper to taste

Instructions:

1. Turn the oven on to 375°F, or 190°C.

2. In a pan, brown ground beef; season with salt and pepper; remove any surplus grease.

3. Arrange sliced eggplant, ground beef, ricotta, mozzarella, and marinara sauce in a baking dish.

4. After layering again, sprinkle Parmesan cheese on top.

5. Bake for thirty minutes, or until brown and bubbling.

6. Add some fresh basil as a garnish before serving.

5. Spinach and Feta Stuffed Chicken Breasts

Total Time: 40 minutes

Cooking Time: 25 minutes

Serves: 2

Ingredients:

- 2 boneless, skinless chicken breasts
- 2 cups fresh spinach, chopped
- 1/2 cup feta cheese, crumbled
- 1 tablespoon olive oil
- Garlic powder, salt, and pepper to taste

Instructions:

1. Turn the oven on to 375°F, or 190°C.

2. Add the chopped spinach to a pan with olive oil and cook until it wilts.

3. Chicken breasts are butterfly-shaped and seasoned with salt, pepper, and garlic powder.

4. Stuff each chicken breast with a mixture of feta and sautéed spinach.

5. Bake the chicken for 25 minutes, or until it is thoroughly done.

6. Cauliflower Fried Rice with Shrimp

Total Time: 25 minutes

Cooking Time: 15 minutes

Serves: 2

Ingredients:

- 2 cups cauliflower rice
- 1/2 pound shrimp, peeled and deveined
- 1 cup mixed vegetables (peas, carrots, corn)
- 2 eggs, beaten
- 2 tablespoons soy sauce
- 1 tablespoon sesame oil
- Green onions for garnish

Instructions:

1. Cook the shrimp in a big pan and set them aside.
2. Cook the cauliflower rice and mixed veggies in the same pan until they are soft.
3. Move the rice aside and add the scrambled eggs to the pan when they have been beaten.
4. Combine eggs, rice, and veggies; mix in cooked shrimp.
5. Add the sesame oil and soy sauce, then top with the green onions.

7. Turkey and Avocado Lettuce Wraps

Total Time: 15 minutes

Cooking Time: 10 minutes

Serves: 2

Ingredients:

- 1/2 pound ground turkey
- 1 teaspoon olive oil
- 1 teaspoon cumin
- 1 teaspoon chili powder
- Iceberg lettuce leaves
- 1 avocado, sliced
- Salsa for topping

Instructions:

1. Heat up some olive oil in a skillet, then add the ground turkey, cumin, and chili powder and cook until browned.

2. Clean and divide the leaves of iceberg lettuce.

3. Spoon combination of turkey onto each leaf of lettuce.

4. Add salsa and sliced avocado on top.

8. Broccoli and Cheddar Stuffed Chicken

Total Time: 35 minutes

Cooking Time: 20 minutes

Serves: 2

Ingredients:

- 2 boneless, skinless chicken breasts
- 1 cup broccoli florets, steamed

- 1/2 cup cheddar cheese, shredded

- 1 teaspoon garlic powder

- Salt and pepper to taste

Instructions:

1. Turn the oven on to 375°F, or 190°C.

2. Add salt, pepper, and garlic powder to chicken breasts for seasoning.

3. On each of the chicken breasts, cut a pocket.

4. Stuff the chicken pockets with a mixture of cheddar cheese and steaming broccoli.

5. Bake the chicken for 20 minutes, or until cooked through.

9. Greek Salad with Grilled Lamb

Total Time: 40 minutes

Cooking Time: 20 minutes

Serves: 2

Ingredients:

- 1 pound lamb chops

- Mixed salad greens

- Cherry tomatoes, halved

- Cucumber, sliced

- Red onion, thinly sliced

- Kalamata olives

- Feta cheese, crumbled

- Greek dressing

Instructions:

1. Set the grill's temperature to medium-high.

2. Once done, grill the lamb chops.

3. Salad greens, tomatoes, cucumber, red onion, olives, and feta should all be combined in a big bowl.

4. Place the grilled lamb slices on.

10. Shrimp and Avocado Salad

Total Time: 20 minutes

Cooking Time: 5 minutes

Serves: 2

Ingredients:

- 1/2 pound shrimp, peeled and deveined

- 1 tablespoon olive oil

- Mixed salad greens

- Avocado, sliced

- Cherry tomatoes, halved

- Red bell pepper, thinly sliced

- Cilantro for garnish

- Lime vinaigrette

Instructions:

1. In a skillet with heated olive oil, sauté shrimp until they turn pink and are fully cooked.

2. Salad greens, avocado slices, cherry tomatoes, and red bell pepper should all be combined in a big bowl.

3. Add some sautéed shrimp to the salad.

4. Over the salad, drizzle some lime vinaigrette and sprinkle some fresh cilantro on top.

11. Buffalo Cauliflower Bites

Total Time: 30 minutes

Cooking Time: 20 minutes

Serves: 4

Ingredients:

- 1 head cauliflower, cut into florets
- 1/2 cup almond flour
- 1/2 cup unsweetened almond milk
- 1 teaspoon garlic powder
- 1/2 cup buffalo sauce
- Ranch dressing for dipping

Instructions:

1. Turn the oven on to 450°F, or 230°C.

2. To make a batter, combine almond flour, almond milk, and garlic powder in a bowl.

3. Place the battered cauliflower florets on a baking sheet after dipping them in it.

4. Bake until golden brown, about 20 minutes.

5. Pour buffalo sauce over the roasted cauliflower.

6. Accompany with ranch dressing for a dip.

12. Caprese Stuffed Avocado

Total Time: 15 minutes

Cooking Time: 0 minutes

Serves: 2

Ingredients:

- 2 avocados, halved and pitted
- Fresh mozzarella balls
- Cherry tomatoes, halved
- Fresh basil leaves
- Balsamic glaze
- Salt and pepper to taste

Instructions:

1. Remove a small amount of avocado from each half to make a bigger well.

2. Stuff the avocado halves with cherry tomatoes, fresh mozzarella, and basil leaves.

3. Season with salt and pepper and drizzle with balsamic glaze.

13. Chicken and Broccoli Stir-Fry

Total Time: 25 minutes

Cooking Time: 15 minutes

Serves: 4

Ingredients:

- 1 pound chicken breast, thinly sliced
- 2 cups broccoli florets
- 1 red bell pepper, sliced
- 1/4 cup soy sauce
- 2 tablespoons sesame oil
- 1 tablespoon ginger, minced
- 2 cloves garlic, minced
- Green onions for garnish

Instructions:

1. Sesame oil should be heated over medium-high heat in a wok or big skillet.
2. Cook the chicken through and brown it by stirring it.
3. Stir-fry the broccoli, bell pepper, ginger, and garlic until the veggies are soft.
4. Over the mixture, drizzle soy sauce and toss until thoroughly mixed.
5. Before serving, garnish with green onions.

14. Turkey and Spinach Stuffed Mushrooms

Total Time: 30 minutes

Cooking Time: 20 minutes

Serves: 3

Ingredients:

- 12 large mushrooms, stems removed

- 1/2 pound ground turkey

- 1 cup fresh spinach, chopped

- 1/2 cup cream cheese

- 1/4 cup Parmesan cheese, grated

- 1 teaspoon Italian seasoning

Instructions:

1. Turn the oven on to 375°F, or 190°C.

2. Cook the ground turkey in a pan until browned.

3. Cook the chopped spinach until it wilts.

4. Combine the turkey mixture, Parmesan, and Italian seasoning in a bowl.

5. After stuffing the mixture into the mushroom caps, bake for 20 minutes.

15. Cabbage and Sausage Skillet

Total Time: 30 minutes

Cooking Time: 20 minutes

Serves: 4

Ingredients:

- 1 pound smoked sausage, sliced

- 1 small cabbage, shredded

- 1 onion, thinly sliced

- 2 cloves garlic, minced

- 1 teaspoon paprika

- Salt and pepper to taste

Instructions:

1. Sausage slices should be cooked till browned in a big skillet.

2. Add the garlic and onions and sauté until softened.

3. Add the shredded cabbage, salt, pepper, and paprika and stir.

4. Cook cabbage, tossing periodically, until it becomes soft.

16. Tuna and Avocado Lettuce Wraps

Total Time: 15 minutes

Cooking Time: 0 minutes

Serves: 2

Ingredients:

- 1 can tuna, drained
- 1 avocado, mashed
- Red onion, finely diced
- Celery, finely chopped
- Lettuce leaves for wrapping
- Lemon juice
- Salt and pepper to taste

Instructions:

1. Combine the mashed avocado, celery, red onion, and drained tuna in a bowl.

2. Add pepper, salt, and lemon juice for seasoning.

3. Place a spoonful of the tuna mixture on each lettuce leaf, then wrap.

17. Grilled Portobello Mushrooms with Pesto

Total Time: 25 minutes

Cooking Time: 15 minutes

Serves: 2

Ingredients:

- 4 large portobello mushrooms
- Olive oil
- Salt and pepper to taste
- Pesto sauce
- Parmesan cheese, grated

Instructions:

1. Set the grill's temperature to medium.
2. After cleaning, season the mushrooms with salt, pepper, and olive oil.
3. On each side, grill the mushrooms for 5 to 7 minutes.
4. After the mushrooms are cooked, cover them with pesto sauce and top with grated Parmesan cheese.

18. Avocado and Bacon Stuffed Chicken

Total Time: 40 minutes

Cooking Time: 25 minutes

Serves: 2

Ingredients:

- 2 boneless, skinless chicken breasts

- 1 avocado, mashed

- 4 slices bacon, cooked and crumbled

- 1/2 cup cheddar cheese, shredded

- Paprika, salt, and pepper to taste

Instructions:

1. Turn the oven on to 375°F, or 190°C.

2. Sprinkle chicken breasts with salt, pepper, and paprika.

3. Create a pocket in each chicken breast and fill it with bacon, cheddar, and mashed avocado.

4. Bake the chicken for 25 minutes, or until it is thoroughly done.

19. Spaghetti Squash with Meatballs

Total Time: 45 minutes

Cooking Time: 30 minutes

Serves: 4

Ingredients:

- 1 medium spaghetti squash, halved and seeds removed

- 1 pound ground beef or turkey

- 1 cup marinara sauce

- 1/4 cup grated Parmesan cheese

- Fresh basil for garnish

- Olive oil

- Salt and pepper to taste

Instructions:

1. Set oven temperature to 400°F, or 200°C.

2. Roast the spaghetti squash halves for 30 minutes after seasoning with salt and pepper and drizzling with olive oil.

3. Form ground meat into meatballs as the squash roasts.

4. Marinara sauce should be used to properly cook meatballs.

5. Using a fork to scrape the spaghetti squash, make "noodles" and add meatballs, marinara, and Parmesan cheese on top.

6. Add some fresh basil as a garnish before serving.

20. Asian-Inspired Beef Stir-Fry

Total Time: 25 minutes

Cooking Time: 15 minutes

Serves: 3

Ingredients:

- 1 pound flank steak, thinly sliced

- 2 cups broccoli florets

- 1 red bell pepper, sliced

- 1 carrot, julienned

- 3 tablespoons soy sauce

- 1 tablespoon oyster sauce

- 1 tablespoon sesame oil

- 2 cloves garlic, minced

- Ginger, grated

- Green onions for garnish

Instructions:

1. Combine the oyster sauce, sesame oil, and soy sauce in a bowl.

2. Stir-fry cut flank steak in a wok or skillet over high heat until browned.

3. Stir-fry the ginger and garlic together.

4. Add the carrot, bell pepper, and broccoli and stir-fry until the veggies are soft.

5. Mix thoroughly after adding the sauce to the stir-fry.

6. Before serving, garnish with green onions.

21. Portobello Mushroom and Goat Cheese Omelette

Total Time: 20 minutes

Cooking Time: 10 minutes

Serves: 2

Ingredients:

- 4 large eggs, beaten

- 2 portobello mushrooms, sliced

- 1/4 cup goat cheese, crumbled

- 1 tablespoon butter

- Fresh chives for garnish

- Salt and pepper to taste

Instructions:

1. Melt butter in a nonstick skillet over medium heat.

2. Cook the sliced mushrooms until they become tender.

3. Cover the mushrooms with beaten eggs, allowing them to firm up a little.

4. Top one side of the omelette with goat cheese crumbles.

5. Once the cheese has melted, fold the omelette in half and continue cooking.

6. Season with salt and pepper and garnish with fresh chives.

22. Keto-friendly Chicken Alfredo with Broccoli

Total Time: 30 minutes

Cooking Time: 20 minutes

Serves: 4

Ingredients:

- 1 pound chicken breasts, diced

- 2 tablespoons olive oil

- 1 cup broccoli florets

- 1 cup heavy cream

- 1/2 cup Parmesan cheese, grated

- 2 cloves garlic, minced

- Salt and pepper to taste

- Fresh parsley for garnish

- Zucchini noodles (optional, for serving)

Instructions:

1. Cook the diced chicken in olive oil in a skillet until it's cooked through.

2. Cook the broccoli until it becomes tender by adding the minced garlic and broccoli florets.

3. Add the heavy cream and mix in the Parmesan cheese until it melts.

4. To taste, add salt and pepper for seasoning.

5. Serve with your preferred low-carb pasta replacement or over zucchini noodles.

6. Before serving, garnish with fresh parsley.

23. Teriyaki Salmon with Cauliflower Rice

Total Time: 25 minutes

Cooking Time: 15 minutes

Serves: 2

Ingredients:

- 2 salmon fillets

- 1/4 cup soy sauce (or tamari for gluten-free)

- 2 tablespoons sugar-free teriyaki sauce

- 1 tablespoon sesame oil

- 2 cups cauliflower rice

- Green onions for garnish

Instructions:

1. Set oven temperature to 400°F, or 200°C.

2. Combine the sugar-free teriyaki sauce and soy sauce in a small bowl.

3. On a baking sheet, arrange the salmon fillets and brush with the teriyaki marinade.

4. Bake the salmon for 15 minutes, or until it is thoroughly cooked.

5. Cook the cauliflower rice in sesame oil in a pan until it becomes soft.

6. Top the teriyaki salmon with cauliflower rice and add some green onions as a garnish.

24. Southwest Chicken Salad

Total Time: 20 minutes

Cooking Time: 15 minutes

Serves: 2

Ingredients:

- 2 boneless, skinless chicken breasts

- 1 tablespoon olive oil

- 1 teaspoon cumin

- 1 teaspoon chili powder

- Mixed salad greens

- Avocado, sliced

- Cherry tomatoes, halved

- Sour cream for dressing

Instructions:

1. Season chicken breasts with salt, pepper, chili powder, and cumin.

2. In a skillet over high heat, fry the chicken until it's done.

3. After slicing, put the chicken aside.

4. Avocado, cherry tomatoes, and salad greens should all be combined in a big bowl.

5. Add sliced chicken over top and cover with sour cream.

25. Pesto Zoodles with Grilled Chicken

Total Time: 30 minutes

Cooking Time: 20 minutes

Serves: 2

Ingredients:

- 2 zucchinis, spiralized
- 2 boneless, skinless chicken breasts
- 1/2 cup pesto sauce
- Cherry tomatoes, halved
- Pine nuts for garnish
- Parmesan cheese, grated

Instructions:

1. Cook the chicken breasts completely on the grill.
2. Cut zucchini into spirals to make zoodles.
3. Heat the pesto sauce in a pan and toss in the zoodles until well warm.
4. Arrange the grilled chicken slices over the pesto zoodles.
5. Add grated Parmesan, pine nuts, and cherry tomatoes as garnish.

26. Egg Drop Soup with Spinach

Total Time: 15 minutes

Cooking Time: 10 minutes

Serves: 2

Ingredients:

- 4 cups chicken broth
- 2 eggs, beaten
- 1 cup fresh spinach
- 2 green onions, sliced
- 1 tablespoon soy sauce
- Sesame oil for drizzling

Instructions:

1. Simmer the chicken broth in a saucepan.
2. Stir gently as you gradually add the beaten eggs to the boiling stock.
3. Cook the fresh spinach until it wilts.
4. Add the cut green onions and soy sauce and stir.
5. Pour some sesame oil over it before serving.

27. Cilantro Lime Shrimp Skewers

Total Time: 20 minutes

Cooking Time: 10 minutes

Serves: 2

Ingredients:

- 1/2 pound shrimp, peeled and deveined
- 2 tablespoons olive oil

- 2 cloves garlic, minced

- Zest and juice of 1 lime

- 2 tablespoons fresh cilantro, chopped

- Salt and pepper to taste

Instructions:

1. Olive oil, minced garlic, lime zest, lime juice, chopped cilantro, salt, and pepper should all be combined in a bowl.

2. After skewering the shrimp, brush them with the cilantro-lime mixture.

3. Shrimp should be cooked through after 3–4 minutes on each side of the grill or skillet.

4. Add additional lime wedges for squeezing to the dish.

28. Cauliflower and Broccoli Gratin

Total Time: 45 minutes

Cooking Time: 25 minutes

Serves: 4

Ingredients:

- 1 head cauliflower, cut into florets

- 1 bunch broccoli, cut into florets

- 1 cup heavy cream

- 1 cup cheddar cheese, shredded

- 1/4 cup Parmesan cheese, grated

- 2 tablespoons butter

- 2 tablespoons almond flour
- Salt and pepper to taste

Instructions:

1. Broccoli and cauliflower should be steamed until barely soft.

2. Melt butter in a skillet, add almond flour, and simmer for one to two minutes.

3. Add heavy cream gradually and whisk until smooth.

4. Add the melted and smooth Parmesan and cheddar cheeses and stir.

5. Add pepper and salt for seasoning.

6. Place the steamed broccoli and cauliflower in a baking dish and top with the cheese sauce.

7. Bake for 20 to 25 minutes, or until brown and bubbling, at 375°F (190°C).

29. Greek Chicken Souvlaki Bowls

Total Time: 30 minutes

Cooking Time: 20 minutes

Serves: 3

Ingredients:

- 1 pound chicken breast, cubed
- 2 tablespoons olive oil
- 1 teaspoon dried oregano
- 1 teaspoon garlic powder
- 1 cucumber, diced

- Cherry tomatoes, halved

- Red onion, thinly sliced

- Feta cheese, crumbled

- Tzatziki sauce

Instructions:

1. Combine the olive oil, oregano, and garlic powder with the chicken cubes in a bowl.

2. After the chicken is well cooked, thread it onto skewers and grill.

3. Put grilled chicken, cherry tomatoes, sliced cucumber, and red onion in bowls.

4. Add some crumbled feta on top and pour some tzatziki sauce over it.

30. Italian Sausage and Pepper Skillet

Total Time: 35 minutes

Cooking Time: 25 minutes

Serves: 4

Ingredients:

- 1 pound Italian sausage, sliced

- 1 bell pepper, sliced

- 1 onion, sliced

- 2 cloves garlic, minced

- 1 can diced tomatoes

- 1 teaspoon Italian seasoning

- Salt and pepper to taste

Instructions:

1. Cook the pieces of Italian sausage over medium heat in a pan.

2. Add the onion, bell pepper slices, and minced garlic; sauté the vegetables until they become tender.

3. Add the diced tomatoes with their juices and season with salt, pepper, and Italian seasoning.

4. Simmer for 15 to 20 minutes, or until sauce thickens and flavors combine.

5. Enjoy while hot!

Snack Recipes

1. Avocado and Bacon Deviled Eggs

Total Time: 20 minutes

Cooking Time: 10 minutes

Serves: 4

Ingredients:

- 4 hard-boiled eggs
- 1 ripe avocado
- 2 slices of cooked bacon, crumbled
- 1 tablespoon mayonnaise
- Salt and pepper to taste

Instructions:

1. Halve the hard-boiled eggs and extract the yolks.

2. Add avocado, bacon, mayonnaise, salt, and pepper to the yolks and mash.

3. Return the mixture to the egg whites with a spoon.

4. Before serving, chill.

2. Zucchini Chips

Total Time: 40 minutes

Cooking Time: 30 minutes

Serves: 2

Ingredients:

- 2 medium zucchinis, thinly sliced
- 2 tablespoons olive oil
- Salt and pepper to taste
- 1/4 cup grated Parmesan cheese

Instructions:

1. Set oven temperature to 400°F, or 200°C.

2. Add salt, pepper, and olive oil to the zucchini slices and toss.

3. Place on a baking pan and top with Parmesan cheese.

4. Bake till crispy, 25–30 minutes.

3. Cucumber and Cream Cheese Bites

Total Time: 15 minutes

Serves: 2

Ingredients:

- 1 cucumber, sliced
- 4 oz cream cheese, softened
- Smoked salmon (optional)
- Fresh dill for garnish

Instructions:

1. Spread cucumber slices with cream cheese.
2. If desired, add smoked salmon on top.
3. Place some fresh dill on top.

4. Buffalo Cauliflower Bites

Total Time: 35 minutes

Cooking Time: 25 minutes

Serves: 4

Ingredients:

- 1 head cauliflower, cut into florets
- 1/2 cup almond flour
- 1/2 cup buffalo sauce
- 2 tablespoons olive oil
- Salt and pepper to taste

Instructions:

1. Turn the oven on to 450°F, or 230°C.
2. Add salt, pepper, olive oil, and almond flour to the cauliflower and toss.

3. Bake until crispy, about 20 to 25 minutes.

4. Serve by tossing with buffalo sauce.

5. Egg Salad Lettuce Wraps

Total Time: 15 minutes

Serves: 2

Ingredients:

- 4 hard-boiled eggs, chopped

- 2 tablespoons mayonnaise

- 1 teaspoon Dijon mustard

- Salt and pepper to taste

- Lettuce leaves for wrapping

Instructions:

1. Combine eggs, mustard, mayonnaise, pepper, and salt.

2. Transfer onto lettuce leaves and enclose.

6. Almond and Cheese Stuffed Jalapeños

Total Time: 25 minutes

Cooking Time: 15 minutes

Serves: 4

Ingredients:

- 8 jalapeños, halved and seeded

- 1/2 cup cream cheese, softened

- 1/4 cup shredded cheddar

- 1/4 cup chopped almonds

Instructions:

1. Combine almonds, cheddar, and cream cheese.

2. Stuff mixture into halves of jalapeños.

3. Bake for fifteen minutes at 375°F (190°C).

7. Greek Yogurt and Berry Parfait

Total Time: 10 minutes

Serves: 2

Ingredients:

- 1 cup Greek yogurt

- 1/2 cup mixed berries (blueberries, strawberries)

- 2 tablespoons crushed nuts (almonds, walnuts)

Instructions:

1. Arrange nuts, berries, and Greek yogurt in a glass.

2. Continue until all of the glass is full.

8. Bacon-wrapped Asparagus

Total Time: 25 minutes

Cooking Time: 15 minutes

Serves: 4

Ingredients:

- 16 asparagus spears

- 8 slices of bacon

- Olive oil
- Salt and pepper to taste

Instructions:

1. Wrap a slice of bacon around each spear of asparagus.

2. Add a drizzle of olive oil and season with pepper and salt.

3. Bake 15 minutes at 400°F (200°C).

9. Tuna Cucumber Boats

Total Time: 15 minutes

Serves: 2

Ingredients:

- 1 can tuna, drained
- 2 tablespoons mayonnaise
- 1 tablespoon Dijon mustard
- 2 cucumbers, halved
- Cherry tomatoes for garnish

Instructions:

1. Combine mustard, mayonnaise, and tuna.

2. Spoon tuna mixture into cucumber halves.

3. Add cherry tomatoes as a garnish.

10. Cheese and Pepperoni Bites

Total Time: 10 minutes

Serves: 2

Ingredients:

- 1 cup mozzarella cheese, cubed
- 1/2 cup pepperoni slices
- Cherry tomatoes for garnish

Instructions:

1. Put slices of pepperoni and mozzarella cubes on skewers.
2. Add cherry tomatoes as a garnish.

11. Spinach and Feta Stuffed Mushrooms

Total Time: 30 minutes

Cooking Time: 20 minutes

Serves: 4

Ingredients:

- 12 large mushrooms, stems removed
- 2 cups fresh spinach, chopped
- 1/2 cup feta cheese, crumbled
- 2 cloves garlic, minced
- Salt and pepper to taste

Instructions:

1. Turn the oven on to 375°F, or 190°C.
2. Combine feta, spinach, garlic, salt, and pepper.
3. After stuffing the mixture into the mushroom caps, bake for 15 to 20 minutes.

12. Chicken Avocado Lettuce Wraps

Total Time: 20 minutes

Cooking Time: 10 minutes

Serves: 2

Ingredients:

- 1 cup cooked chicken, shredded
- 1 ripe avocado, diced
- 2 tablespoons mayonnaise
- 1 tablespoon lime juice
- Lettuce leaves for wrapping

Instructions:

1. Mix avocado, mayonnaise, lime juice, and chicken.
2. Transfer onto lettuce leaves and enclose.

13. Mini Caprese Skewers

Total Time: 15 minutes

Serves: 4

Ingredients:

- Cherry tomatoes
- Fresh mozzarella balls
- Basil leaves
- Balsamic glaze for drizzling

Instructions:

1. Put basil leaves, mozzarella balls, and cherry tomatoes on skewers.

2. Before serving, drizzle with balsamic glaze.

14. Smoked Salmon Cucumber Rolls

Total Time: 15 minutes

Serves: 2

Ingredients:

- 4 oz smoked salmon
- 1 cucumber, thinly sliced
- Cream cheese
- Chives for garnish

Instructions:

1. Spread cucumber slices with cream cheese.
2. Top with smoked salmon and roll.
3. Sprinkle chives on top.

15. Almond Butter Celery Sticks

Total Time: 10 minutes

Serves: 2

Ingredients:

- Celery sticks
- Almond butter
- Sliced strawberries for topping

Instructions:

1. Spread celery sticks with almond butter.

2. Add sliced strawberries on top.

16. Keto Guacamole with Jicama Sticks

Total Time: 15 minutes

Serves: 4

Ingredients:

- 3 ripe avocados, mashed
- 1/4 cup diced red onion
- 1/4 cup chopped cilantro
- 1 lime, juiced
- Jicama sticks for dipping

Instructions:

1. Add lime juice, red onion, cilantro, and avocados.
2. Add jicama sticks for dipping.

17. Parmesan Crisps

Total Time: 15 minutes

Cooking Time: 10 minutes

Serves: 4

Ingredients:

- 1 cup grated Parmesan cheese
- 1 teaspoon Italian seasoning

Instructions:

1. Turn the oven on to 375°F, or 190°C.

2. Place little heaps of Parmesan cheese onto a baking sheet.

3. After adding some Italian spice, bake for 8 to 10 minutes, or until crispy.

18. Tofu and Veggie Skewers

Total Time: 30 minutes

Cooking Time: 15 minutes

Serves: 4

Ingredients:

- 1 block firm tofu, cubed
- Cherry tomatoes
- Bell pepper chunks
- Zucchini slices
- Olive oil
- Garlic powder, salt, and pepper to taste

Instructions:

1. Put vegetables and tofu on skewers.

2. Apply a thin layer of olive oil and season with salt, pepper, and garlic powder.

3. Fry or bake the tofu until it turns golden.

19. Keto-friendly Trail Mix

Total Time: 10 minutes

Serves: 4

Ingredients:

- 1/2 cup almonds
- 1/2 cup walnuts
- 1/4 cup pumpkin seeds
- 1/4 cup unsweetened coconut flakes
- Dark chocolate chips (use sparingly)

Instructions:

1. In a bowl, combine all ingredients.
2. Divide into servings the size of snacks.

20. Cabbage and Sausage Bites

Total Time: 25 minutes

Cooking Time: 15 minutes

Serves: 4

Ingredients:

- 1/2 head of cabbage, cut into wedges
- 8 sausages, sliced
- Olive oil
- Paprika, salt, and pepper to taste

Instructions:

1. Combine sausage pieces and cabbage wedges with olive oil.
2. Add paprika, salt, and pepper to taste.
3. Roast for fifteen minutes at 400°F (200°C) in the oven.

Dessert Recipes

1. Chocolate Avocado Mousse

Total Time: 15 minutes

Cooking Time: 5 minutes

Serves: 4

Ingredients:

- 2 ripe avocados
- 1/4 cup unsweetened cocoa powder
- 1/4 cup almond milk
- 1/4 cup powdered erythritol
- 1 teaspoon vanilla extract

Instructions:

1. Avocados, almond milk, erythritol, cocoa powder, and vanilla extract should all be combined in a blender.
2. Blend till creamy and smooth.
3. Before serving, place in the refrigerator for at least one hour.

2. Keto Berry Cheesecake Bites

Total Time: 2 hours

Cooking Time: 30 minutes

Serves: 8

Ingredients:

- 1 cup almond flour

- 4 tablespoons butter, melted

- 8 oz cream cheese, softened

- 1/2 cup powdered erythritol

- 1 teaspoon vanilla extract

- 1 cup mixed berries (strawberries, blueberries, raspberries)

Instructions:

1. Combine melted butter with almond flour and press into a pan to form a crust.

2. Beat cream cheese, erythritol, and vanilla together until smooth in a another bowl.

3. Cover the crust with the cream cheese mixture.

4. After adding a layer of mixed berries, chill for a minimum of sixty minutes.

3. Coconut Almond Balls

Total Time: 30 minutes

Cooking Time: 10 minutes

Serves: 12

Ingredients:

- 1 cup unsweetened shredded coconut

- 1 cup almond flour

- 1/4 cup coconut oil, melted

- 1/4 cup powdered erythritol

- 1 teaspoon almond extract

Instructions:

1. In a bowl, combine erythritol, almond extract, melted coconut oil, almond flour, and shredded coconut.

2. Shape into little balls and transfer to a dish lined with parchment paper.

3. Place in the fridge for 20 minutes prior to serving.

4. Lemon Cheesecake Fat Bombs

Total Time: 1 hour

Cooking Time: 15 minutes

Serves: 10

Ingredients:

- 8 oz cream cheese, softened

- 1/4 cup butter, softened

- 1/4 cup powdered erythritol

- 1 teaspoon lemon zest

- 1 tablespoon lemon juice

Instructions:

1. Cream cheese and butter should be smoothed out.

2. Pour in the lemon juice, zest, and erythritol. Blend thoroughly.

3. Transfer into molds or shape into tiny balls, then chill until solid.

5. Almond Flour Chocolate Chip Cookies

Total Time: 25 minutes

Cooking Time: 12 minutes

Serves: 12

Ingredients:

- 2 cups almond flour

- 1/2 cup butter, softened

- 1/2 cup powdered erythritol

- 1 teaspoon vanilla extract

- 1/2 cup sugar-free chocolate chips

Instructions:

1. Set oven temperature to 175°C/350°F.

2. Blend together almond flour, vanilla extract, erythritol, and softened butter.

3. After adding the chocolate chips, shape into cookies.

4. Bake until brown along the edges, about 12 minutes.

6. Peanut Butter Fat Bombs

Total Time: 1 hour

Cooking Time: 10 minutes

Serves: 8

Ingredients:

- 1/2 cup natural peanut butter

- 1/4 cup coconut oil, melted

- 2 tablespoons powdered erythritol
- 1/2 teaspoon vanilla extract
- Pinch of salt

Instructions:

1. Combine peanut butter, erythritol, melted coconut oil, vanilla essence, and a small amount of salt.
2. Transfer into molds or form into little balls.
3. Prior to serving, freeze for thirty minutes.

7. Vanilla Chia Seed Pudding

Total Time: 4 hours

Cooking Time: 5 minutes

Serves: 4

Ingredients:

- 1 cup unsweetened almond milk
- 1/4 cup chia seeds
- 1/4 cup powdered erythritol
- 1 teaspoon vanilla extract

Instructions:

1. Blend together almond milk, erythritol, chia seeds, and vanilla essence.
2. Place in the refrigerator for four hours or overnight.
3. Before serving, give it a good stir.

8. Cinnamon Roll Mug Cake

Total Time: 10 minutes

Cooking Time: 5 minutes

Serves: 1

Ingredients:

- 3 tablespoons almond flour

- 1 tablespoon melted butter

- 1/2 teaspoon baking powder

- 1 teaspoon powdered erythritol

- 1/2 teaspoon cinnamon

- 1 egg

Instructions:

1. In a mug, combine almond flour, butter that has melted, egg, baking powder, erythritol, and cinnamon.

2. For 90 seconds, or until set, microwave.

3. Before serving, allow it to cool for one minute.

9. Chocolate Coconut Truffles

Total Time: 1 hour

Cooking Time: 10 minutes

Serves: 10

Ingredients:

- 1/2 cup unsweetened shredded coconut

- 2 tablespoons cocoa powder

- 2 tablespoons coconut oil, melted
- 1 tablespoon powdered erythritol
- 1/2 teaspoon vanilla extract

Instructions:

1. Combine erythritol, melted coconut oil, chocolate powder, shredded coconut, and vanilla essence.

2. Shape into tiny truffles and chill until solid.

10. Raspberry Almond Crisp

Total Time: 45 minutes

Cooking Time: 30 minutes

Serves: 6

Ingredients:

- 2 cups raspberries
- 1 cup almond flour
- 1/4 cup sliced almonds
- 1/4 cup melted butter
- 1/4 cup powdered erythritol
- 1 teaspoon vanilla extract

Instructions:

1. Set oven temperature to 175°C/350°F.

2. Place raspberries in a baking dish and toss with vanilla extract and erythritol.

3. Almond flour, melted butter, chopped almonds, and a dash of salt should all be combined in a bowl.

4. After the raspberries, scatter the almond mixture on top.

5. Bake until the top is golden brown, about 30 minutes.

11. Almond Butter Chocolate Cups

Total Time: 1 hour

Cooking Time: 15 minutes

Serves: 8

Ingredients:

- 1/2 cup almond butter

- 1/4 cup coconut oil, melted

- 2 tablespoons cocoa powder

- 2 tablespoons powdered erythritol

- 1/2 teaspoon vanilla extract

Instructions:

1. Blend together almond butter, erythritol, cocoa powder, and heated coconut oil with vanilla extract.

2. Transfer the blend into silicone molds or cupcake liners.

3. Before serving, freeze for forty-five minutes.

12. Pumpkin Spice Cheesecake Bites

Total Time: 2 hours

Cooking Time: 30 minutes

Serves: 10

Ingredients:

- 8 oz cream cheese, softened

- 1/2 cup canned pumpkin

- 1/4 cup powdered erythritol

- 1 teaspoon pumpkin spice

- 1 teaspoon vanilla extract

Instructions:

1. Add vanilla essence, pumpkin spice, erythritol, and cream cheese and beat until smooth.

2. Pour the mixture into ice cube trays or molds using a spoon.

3. For at least one and a half hours, refrigerate.

13. Blueberry Almond Mug Cake

Total Time: 10 minutes

Cooking Time: 5 minutes

Serves: 1

Ingredients:

- 3 tablespoons almond flour

- 1 tablespoon melted butter

- 1/2 teaspoon baking powder

- 1 tablespoon powdered erythritol

- 1/4 cup blueberries

- 1 egg

Instructions:

1. In a mug, stir together almond flour, melted butter, erythritol, baking powder, blueberries, and egg.

2. For 90 seconds, or until set, microwave.

3. Before serving, allow it to cool for one minute.

14. Chocolate Mint Avocado Pudding

Total Time: 15 minutes

Cooking Time: 5 minutes

Serves: 4

Ingredients:

- 2 ripe avocados

- 1/4 cup unsweetened cocoa powder

- 1/4 cup almond milk

- 1/4 cup powdered erythritol

- 1/2 teaspoon peppermint extract

Instructions:

1. Blend together avocados, erythritol, almond milk, cocoa powder, and peppermint essence in a blender.

2. Blend till creamy and smooth.

3. Before serving, place in the refrigerator for at least one hour.

15. Strawberry Coconut Popsicles

Total Time: 6 hours

Freezing Time: 4-6 hours

Serves: 6

Ingredients:

- 1 cup strawberries, hulled and sliced

- 1 cup coconut milk

- 1/4 cup powdered erythritol

- 1 teaspoon vanilla extract

Instructions:

1. Smoothly blend erythritol, coconut milk, strawberries, and vanilla essence.

2. Fill popsicle molds, then freeze for solidification.

16. Hazelnut Chocolate Truffles

Total Time: 1 hour

Cooking Time: 10 minutes

Serves: 12

Ingredients:

- 1/2 cup hazelnut meal

- 2 tablespoons cocoa powder

- 2 tablespoons coconut oil, melted

- 2 tablespoons powdered erythritol

- 1/2 teaspoon vanilla extract

Instructions:

1. Combine erythritol, melted coconut oil, hazelnut meal, cocoa powder, and vanilla essence.

2. Shape into tiny truffles and chill until solid.

17. Lemon Coconut Bars

Total Time: 1.5 hours

Cooking Time: 40 minutes

Serves: 9

Ingredients:

- 1 cup almond flour

- 1/4 cup coconut flour

- 1/2 cup melted butter

- 1/4 cup powdered erythritol

- 3 eggs

- Zest and juice of 2 lemons

Instructions:

1. Combine erythritol, melted butter, coconut flour, almond flour, and one beaten egg.

2. To create a crust, press the mixture into a baking dish.

3. Whisk the remaining eggs, lemon zest, and lemon juice in a another basin.

4. Cover the crust with the lemon mixture and bake for 30 to 40 minutes at 350°F/175°C.

18. Chocolate Hazelnut Chia Pudding

Total Time: 4 hours

Cooking Time: 5 minutes

Serves: 4

Ingredients:

- 1 cup unsweetened almond milk
- 1/4 cup chia seeds
- 2 tablespoons cocoa powder
- 2 tablespoons powdered erythritol
- 1/2 teaspoon hazelnut extract

Instructions:

1. Combine erythritol, cocoa powder, chia seeds, almond milk, and hazelnut essence.
2. Place in the refrigerator for four hours or overnight.
3. Before serving, give it a good stir.

19. Raspberry Almond Scones

Total Time: 30 minutes

Cooking Time: 15 minutes

Serves: 8

Ingredients:

- 2 cups almond flour
- 1/4 cup melted butter
- 1/4 cup powdered erythritol

- 1/2 teaspoon almond extract
- 1/2 cup fresh raspberries

Instructions:

1. Combine erythritol, almond extract, melted butter, and almond flour.

2. Fold in the fresh raspberries gently.

3. Shape into scones and bake for 15 minutes at 350°F/175°C.

20. Vanilla Almond Panna Cotta

Total Time: 4 hours

Cooking Time: 10 minutes

Serves: 4

Ingredients:

- 1 cup almond milk
- 1 teaspoon gelatin
- 1/4 cup powdered erythritol
- 1 teaspoon vanilla extract
- Slivered almonds for garnish

Instructions:

1. Warm up some almond milk, then add the gelatin and let it sit for a few minutes.

2. After mixing until erythritol is dissolved, stir in vanilla essence.

3. Transfer into serving glasses and keep chilled for a minimum of four hours.

4. Before serving, garnish with slivered almonds.

Smoothies Recipes

1. Berry Bliss

Total Time: 5 minutes

Cooking Time: 0 minutes

Serves: 1

Ingredients:

- 1/2 cup frozen strawberries
- 1/4 cup frozen blueberries
- 1/4 cup unsweetened almond milk
- 1/4 cup Greek yogurt (full-fat)
- 1 tablespoon almond butter
- Ice cubes (optional)

Instructions:

1. In blender, combine all ingredients.
2. Blend till creamy and smooth.
3. If desired, add some ice cubes.
4. After pouring into a glass, savor!

2. Green Goddess

Total Time: 7 minutes

Cooking Time: 0 minutes

Serves: 1

Ingredients:

- 1/2 cup spinach leaves
- 1/4 avocado
- 1/4 cup cucumber, chopped
- 1/2 cup unsweetened coconut milk
- 1 tablespoon chia seeds
- Stevia or erythritol to taste
- Ice cubes (optional)

Instructions:

1. Spinach, avocado, cucumber, and coconut milk should all be thoroughly blended.
2. Blend in the sweetener and chia seeds once more.
3. If desired, add ice cubes and process until smooth.
4. Pour into a glass, then savor the delicious green flavor!

3. Chocolate Almond Delight

Total Time: 8 minutes

Cooking Time: 2 minutes

Serves: 1

Ingredients:

- 1 cup unsweetened almond milk
- 2 tablespoons unsweetened cocoa powder
- 1/4 cup almond flour

- 1/2 teaspoon vanilla extract
- 1 tablespoon sugar-free chocolate syrup
- Ice cubes (optional)

Instructions:

1. Almond milk is reheated for two minutes in the microwave.
2. Blend together chocolate syrup, almond flour, vanilla extract, and cocoa powder in a blender.
3. Warm almond milk should be added to a blender, then processed until smooth.
4. If desired, add ice cubes and mix one more.
5. Pour into a glass and enjoy the delicious chocolate flavor.

4. Tropical Paradise

Total Time: 6 minutes

Cooking Time: 0 minutes

Serves: 1

Ingredients:

- 1/2 cup frozen pineapple chunks
- 1/4 cup coconut cream
- 1/4 cup unsweetened almond milk
- 1/4 cup full-fat Greek yogurt
- 1 tablespoon chia seeds
- Stevia or erythritol to taste
- Ice cubes (optional)

Instructions:

1. Puree the pineapple, yogurt, almond milk, and coconut cream until smooth.

2. Blend in the sweetener and chia seeds once more.

3. If preferred, add ice cubes and mix until smooth.

4. Pour into a glass to take a trip to an idyllic tropical place!

5. Minty Fresh

Total Time: 5 minutes

Cooking Time: 0 minutes

Serves: 1

Ingredients:

*   1/2 cup fresh spinach leaves

*   1/4 cup fresh mint leaves

*   1/2 avocado

*   1/4 cup unsweetened almond milk

*   1/4 cup full-fat Greek yogurt

*   Stevia or erythritol to taste

*   Ice cubes (optional)

Instructions:

1. Mint, avocado, spinach, almond milk, and yogurt should all be properly blended.

2. Blend once more after adding sweetener to taste.

3. If desired, add ice cubes and process until smooth.

4. Pour into a glass, then savor the cool, minty taste.

6. Peanut Butter Banana Bliss

Total Time: 6 minutes

Cooking Time: 0 minutes

Serves: 1

Ingredients:

- 1/2 banana

- 1 tablespoon natural peanut butter

- 1/4 cup unsweetened almond milk

- 1/4 cup full-fat Greek yogurt

- 1/2 teaspoon vanilla extract

- Ice cubes (optional)

Instructions:

1. Smoothly blend banana, yogurt, peanut butter, almond milk, and vanilla extract.

2. If desired, add ice cubes and mix one more.

3. Pour into a glass, then savor the blissful creamy peanut butter banana.

7. Orange Creamsicle

Total Time: 5 minutes

Cooking Time: 0 minutes

Serves: 1

Ingredients:

- 1/2 cup unsweetened almond milk
- 1/4 cup heavy cream
- 1/2 orange, peeled
- 1/4 teaspoon vanilla extract
- Stevia or erythritol to taste
- Ice cubes (optional)

Instructions:

1. Orange juice, heavy cream, almond milk, and vanilla essence should all be thoroughly blended.
2. Blend once more after adding sweetener to taste.
3. If preferred, add ice cubes and mix until smooth.
4. Pour into a glass and savor the flavor of an orange creamsicle that brings back memories.

8. Cinnamon Roll Delight

Total Time: 7 minutes

Cooking Time: 2 minutes

Serves: 1

Ingredients:

- 1 cup unsweetened almond milk
- 1/2 teaspoon ground cinnamon
- 1/4 teaspoon vanilla extract
- 1 tablespoon almond flour

- 1 tablespoon cream cheese

- Stevia or erythritol to taste

- Ice cubes (optional)

Instructions:

1. Almond milk is reheated for two minutes in the microwave.

2. Blend together almond flour, cream cheese, cinnamon, and vanilla essence in a blender with heated almond milk.

3. Blend till smooth after adding sweetener to taste.

4. If desired, add ice cubes and mix one more.

5. Transfer to a glass and enjoy the sweetness of a cinnamon roll treat.

9. Blueberry Lemon Zest

Total Time: 6 minutes

Cooking Time: 0 minutes

Serves: 1

Ingredients:

- 1/2 cup frozen blueberries

- Zest of 1 lemon

- 1/4 cup unsweetened almond milk

- 1/4 cup full-fat Greek yogurt

- 1 tablespoon chia seeds

- Stevia or erythritol to taste

- Ice cubes (optional)

Instructions:

1. Mix the yogurt, chia seeds, almond milk, blueberries, and zest of the lemon until thoroughly blended.

2. Blend once more after adding sweetener to taste.

3. If desired, add ice cubes and process until smooth.

4. Pour into a glass, then savor the lemon and blueberry flavors that explode.

10. Avocado Lime Refresher

Total Time: 5 minutes

Cooking Time: 0 minutes

Serves: 1

Ingredients:

- 1/2 avocado

- Juice of 1 lime

- 1/4 cup unsweetened almond milk

- 1/4 cup full-fat Greek yogurt

- Stevia or erythritol to taste

- Ice cubes (optional)

Instructions:

1. Avocado, yogurt, almond milk, and lime juice are blended till.

Nutritional Info of all Recipes

1. Grilled Chicken Caesar Salad

Total Time: 30 minutes

Cooking Time: 20 minutes

Serves: 4

Ingredients:

- 4 boneless, skinless chicken breasts
- Romaine lettuce, chopped
- Parmesan cheese, grated
- Caesar dressing (low-carb)

Instructions:

1. Grill at a medium-high temperature.
2. Add salt and pepper to chicken breasts for seasoning.
3. Chicken should be cooked thoroughly after 10 minutes on each side of the grill.
4. Serve grilled chicken slices on top of chopped Romaine lettuce.
5. Drizzle with Caesar dressing and top with Parmesan cheese.
6. Details about Nutrition (per serving):
7. 350 calories, 40g of protein, 15g of fat, 5g of carbs, and 2g of fiber.

2. Zucchini Noodles with Pesto

Total Time: 25 minutes

Cooking Time: 15 minutes

Serves: 3

Ingredients:

- 3 medium zucchinis, spiralized

- 1 cup cherry tomatoes, halved

- 1/2 cup pesto sauce (low-carb)

Instructions:

1. In a pan set over medium heat, warm the olive oil.

2. Zoodles should be sautéed for 5 to 7 minutes to become soft.

3. Cook for a further two to three minutes after adding the cherry tomatoes.

4. Serve after tossing with pesto sauce.

5. Details about Nutrition (per serving):

6. Total calories: 250; fat: 20g; protein: 5g; carbohydrates: 10g; fiber: 4g.

3. Baked Salmon with Lemon and Dill

Total Time: 25 minutes

Cooking Time: 15 minutes

Serves: 2

Ingredients:

- 2 salmon fillets

- 2 tablespoons olive oil

- 1 lemon, sliced

- Fresh dill, chopped

- Salt and pepper to taste

Instructions:

1. Turn the oven on to 400°F, or 200°C.

2. Salmon fillets should be put on a baking pan.

3. Drizzle with olive oil, sprinkle with salt and pepper, then garnish with dill and lemon slices.

4. Bake the salmon for 12 to 15 minutes, or until it flake easily.

5. Details about Nutrition (per serving):

6. 300 calories, 25g of protein, 20g of fat, 2g of carbs, and 0g of fiber.

4. Spinach and Feta Stuffed Chicken Breast

Total Time: 40 minutes

Cooking Time: 25 minutes

Serves: 4

Ingredients:

*   4 boneless, skinless chicken breasts

*   2 cups fresh spinach, chopped

*   1/2 cup feta cheese, crumbled

*   Garlic powder, salt, and pepper to taste

Instructions:

1. Turn the oven on to 375°F, or 190°C.

2. Chicken breasts are butterfly-shaped and seasoned with salt, pepper, and garlic powder.

3. Place feta and chopped spinach inside each chicken breast.

4. Put toothpicks through the chicken and bake for 20 to 25 minutes, or until cooked through.

5. Details about Nutrition (per serving):

6. 280 calories, 35g of protein, 12g of fat, 3g of carbs, and 1g of fiber.

5. Cauliflower Mash

Total Time: 20 minutes

Cooking Time: 15 minutes

Serves: 4

Ingredients:

- 1 medium cauliflower, cut into florets

- 2 tablespoons butter

- 1/4 cup heavy cream

- Salt and pepper to taste

Instructions:

1. Steam or boil cauliflower until it becomes soft.

2. After draining, mix until smooth with butter, heavy cream, salt, and pepper.

3. Taste and adjust seasoning and consistency.

4. Details about Nutrition (per serving):

5. 120 calories; 3g of protein; 10g of fat; 6g of carbohydrates; and 3g of fiber

6. Avocado and Bacon Egg Cups

Total Time: 30 minutes

Cooking Time: 20 minutes

Serves: 3

Ingredients:

- 3 avocados, halved and pitted
- 6 eggs
- 6 slices bacon, cooked and crumbled
- Salt and pepper to taste
- Chopped chives for garnish

Instructions:

1. Turn the oven on to 375°F, or 190°C.
2. To create space for the eggs, scoop out part of the avocado flesh.
3. Arrange the avocados on a baking sheet and split each one in half.
4. Add some salt, pepper, and bacon crumbs for seasoning.
5. Bake the eggs for 15 to 20 minutes, or until done to your preference.
6. Before serving, garnish with finely chopped chives.
7. Details about Nutrition (per serving):
8. 300 calories; 12g of protein; 25g of fat; 8g of carbohydrates; and 5g of fiber

7. Beef and Broccoli Stir-Fry

Total Time: 25 minutes

Cooking Time: 15 minutes

Serves: 4

Ingredients:

- 1 lb flank steak, thinly sliced

- 3 cups broccoli florets

- 2 tablespoons soy sauce (low-carb)

- 1 tablespoon olive oil

- Garlic powder, ginger, and pepper to taste

Instructions:

1. In a wok or skillet, warm up the olive oil over medium-high heat.

2. Stir-fry the steak slices until they turn brown.

3. When the broccoli is crisp-tender, add it and stir-fry it some more.

4. Add pepper, ginger powder, garlic powder, and soy sauce for seasoning.

5. Details about Nutrition (per serving):

6. 350 calories, 30g of protein, 20g of fat, 8g of carbohydrates, and 3g of fiber

8. Eggplant Lasagna

Total Time: 1 hour

Cooking Time: 40 minutes

Serves: 6

Ingredients:

- 1 large eggplant, thinly sliced lengthwise

- 1 lb ground beef

- 2 cups marinara sauce (low-carb)

- 2 cups ricotta cheese

- 2 cups mozzarella cheese, shredded

- Fresh basil for garnish

Instructions:

1. Turn the oven on to 375°F, or 190°C.

2. Bake or grill slices of eggplant until they are soft.

3. Brown ground beef in a skillet and stir in marinara sauce.

4. Arrange the eggplant, meat sauce, mozzarella, and ricotta in a baking dish.

5. Continue layering, and then top with a layer of cheese.

6. Bake for twenty to thirty minutes, or until brown and bubbling.

7. Details about Nutrition (per serving):

8. 400 calories Protein

9. Salmon and Asparagus Foil Packets

Total Time: 30 minutes

Cooking Time: 20 minutes

Serves: 2

Ingredients:

- 2 salmon fillets

- 1 bunch asparagus, trimmed

- 2 tablespoons olive oil

- Lemon slices

- Salt and pepper to taste

Instructions:

1. Turn the oven on to 400°F, or 200°C.

2. Line a piece of foil with each salmon fillet.

3. Place the asparagus next to the fish.

4. Add lemon slices, drizzle with olive oil, and season with salt and pepper.

5. Bake the foil-sealed packages for 15 to 20 minutes.

6. Details about Nutrition (per serving):

7. 320 calories; 30g of protein; 20g of fat; 6g of carbohydrates; and 3g of fiber

10. Turkey and Cheese Stuffed Bell Peppers

Total Time: 45 minutes

Cooking Time: 30 minutes

Serves: 4

Ingredients:

- 4 bell peppers, halved and seeds removed

- 1 lb ground turkey

- 1 cup shredded cheddar cheese

- 1 cup cauliflower rice

- 1 cup salsa (low-carb)

- Taco seasoning to taste

Instructions:

1. Turn the oven on to 375°F, or 190°C.

2. After browning the turkey, add taco spice.

3. Add salsa and cauliflower rice and stir.

4. Spoon the turkey mixture into each side of a bell pepper.

5. Add shredded cheddar cheese on top.

6. Bake peppers for 25 to 30 minutes, or until soft.

7. Details about Nutrition (per serving):

8. 280 calories, 25g protein, 15g fat, 10g carbs, and 3g fiber.

11. Cabbage and Ground Beef Skillet

Total Time: 30 minutes

Cooking Time: 20 minutes

Serves: 4

Ingredients:

- 1 lb ground beef

- 1 small head cabbage, shredded

- 1 onion, diced

- 2 cloves garlic, minced

- 1 can diced tomatoes (no sugar added)

- Salt, pepper, and paprika to taste

Instructions:

1. Brown ground meat, onions, and garlic in a big skillet.

2. Cook the shredded cabbage until it wilts.

3. Add the diced tomatoes and season with paprika, salt, and pepper.

4. Simmer for ten to fifteen minutes.

5. Details about Nutrition (per serving):

6. 320 calories, 20g of protein, 25g of fat, 10g of carbs, and 4g of fiber.

12. Cauliflower and Broccoli Gratin

Total Time: 40 minutes

Cooking Time: 25 minutes

Serves: 6

Ingredients:

- 1 head cauliflower, cut into florets

- 2 cups broccoli florets

- 1 cup heavy cream

- 1 cup shredded cheddar cheese

- 2 tablespoons butter

- Salt and pepper to taste

Instructions:

1. Broccoli and cauliflower should be steamed till soft.

2. Heat the heavy cream in a saucepan and then stir in the butter.

3. Add cheddar cheese and stir until smooth.

4. Mix the cheese sauce with the veggies, add some seasoning, and put it into a baking dish.

5. Bake for 20 to 25 minutes, or until brown and bubbling.

6. Details about Nutrition (per serving):

7. 280 calories, 10g of protein, 25g of fat, 8g of carbs, and 3g of fiber.

13. Shrimp and Avocado Salad

Total Time: 20 minutes

Cooking Time: 10 minutes

Serves: 2

Ingredients:

- 1 lb shrimp, peeled and deveined

- 2 avocados, diced

- Cherry tomatoes, halved

- Cilantro, chopped

- Lime juice

- Salt and pepper to taste

Instructions:

1. Add some salt and pepper to the shrimp.

2. Fry shrimp in a skillet for two to three minutes on each side.

3. Shrimp, chopped avocados, cherry tomatoes, and cilantro should all be combined in a bowl.

4. Pour in some lime juice and stir lightly.

5. Details about Nutrition (per serving):

6. Total calories: 320; fat: 20; protein: 25; carbohydrates: 12; fiber: 8;

14. Egg Salad Lettuce Wraps

Total Time: 15 minutes

Cooking Time: 10 minutes

Serves: 4

Ingredients:

- 8 hard-boiled eggs, chopped

- 1/2 cup mayonnaise (low-carb)

- 1 tablespoon Dijon mustard

- Celery, finely chopped

- Lettuce leaves for wrapping

Instructions:

1. Combine chopped eggs, celery, and Dijon mustard with mayonnaise.

2. Place egg salad onto leaves of lettuce.

3. Roll, then use toothpicks to secure.

4. Details about Nutrition (per serving):

5. 250 calories, 15g of protein, 20g of fat, 3g of carbs, and 1g of fiber.

15. Cajun Chicken and Bell Pepper Skewers

Total Time: 25 minutes

Cooking Time: 15 minutes

Serves: 4

Ingredients:

- 1 lb chicken breast, cut into chunks

- Bell peppers, assorted colors, cut into chunks

- 2 tablespoons Cajun seasoning

- Olive oil

- Wooden skewers, soaked in water

Instructions:

1. Heat a grill pan or grill.

2. Combine olive oil and Cajun seasoning and toss with chicken and bell peppers.

3. Place onto skewers and cook, rotating regularly, for 10 to 12 minutes.

4. Details about Nutrition (per serving):

5. 280 calories, 30g of protein, 15g of fat, 8g of carbs, and 2g of fiber.

16. Mushroom and Swiss Cheese Omelette

Total Time: 15 minutes

Cooking Time: 10 minutes

Serves: 2

Ingredients:

- 4 eggs, beaten

- 1 cup mushrooms, sliced

- 1/2 cup Swiss cheese, shredded

- Butter

- Salt and pepper to taste

Instructions:

1. Sauté mushrooms in butter in a skillet until they are soft.

2. Cover the mushrooms with whisked eggs.

3. After adding Swiss cheese, fry the eggs until they are set.

4. Add salt and pepper for seasoning, fold, and serve.

5. Details about Nutrition (per serving):

6. 300 calories, 18g of protein, 25g of fat, 4g of carbs, and 1g of fiber.

17. Caprese Salad with Balsamic Glaze

Total Time: 15 minutes

Preparation Time: 15 minutes

Serves: 4

Ingredients:

- 2 cups cherry tomatoes, halved

- 1 cup fresh mozzarella balls

- Fresh basil leaves

- 2 tablespoons extra-virgin olive oil

- 2 tablespoons balsamic glaze

- Salt and pepper to taste

Instructions:

1. Cherry tomatoes, fresh mozzarella balls, and fresh basil leaves should all be combined in a bowl.

2. Drizzle with balsamic glaze and extra virgin olive oil.

3. Add salt and pepper to taste, then gently toss to mix.

4. Details about Nutrition (per serving):

5. 200 calories, 10g of protein, 15g of fat, 8g of carbs, and 2g of fiber.

18. Spaghetti Squash with Meatballs

Total Time: 50 minutes

Cooking Time: 40 minutes

Serves: 4

Ingredients:

- 1 medium spaghetti squash, halved and seeded
- 1 lb ground beef or turkey
- 1 cup marinara sauce (low-carb)
- 1/2 cup grated Parmesan cheese
- Italian seasoning, salt, and pepper to taste

Instructions:

1. Turn the oven on to 375°F, or 190°C.
2. Roast the halves of the spaghetti squash for forty minutes, cut side down.
3. Brown ground beef or turkey in a skillet and season with salt, pepper, and Italian seasoning.
4. Add marinara sauce and bring to a simmer.
5. Scrape the spaghetti squash with a fork to create strands.
6. Top spaghetti squash with meatballs and top with Parmesan cheese.
7. Details about Nutrition (per serving):
8. 350 calories, 25g of protein, 20g of fat, 12g of carbs, and 3g of fiber.

19. Cucumber and Cream Cheese Roll-Ups

Total Time: 10 minutes

Preparation Time: 10 minutes

Serves: 2

Ingredients:

- 1 large cucumber, thinly sliced lengthwise

- 1/2 cup cream cheese, softened

- Smoked salmon or deli meat slices

- Chopped chives for garnish

Instructions:

1. Arrange the pieces of cucumber.

2. On each piece, spread a little cream cheese.

3. Top with a slice of deli meat or smoked salmon.

4. Roll, then use toothpicks to secure.

5. Sprinkle chopped chives over top.

6. Details about Nutrition (per serving):

7. 180 calories, 8g of protein, 15g of fat, 5g of carbs, and 1g of fiber.

20. Lemon Garlic Butter Shrimp

Total Time: 20 minutes

Cooking Time: 10 minutes

Serves: 3

Ingredients:

- 1 lb large shrimp, peeled and deveined

- 3 tablespoons butter

- 3 cloves garlic, minced

- Juice of 1 lemon

- Fresh parsley, chopped

- Salt and pepper to taste

Instructions:

1. Melt butter in a skillet over a medium heat.

2. When aromatic, add the minced garlic and sauté it.

3. Add the shrimp and cook for 2 to 3 minutes on each side, or until pink.

4. Add a squeeze of lemon juice, chopped parsley, salt, and pepper to the shrimp.

5. Details about Nutrition (per serving):

6. 250 calories, 20g of protein, 18g of fat, 3g of carbs, and 0g of fiber.

21. Turkey and Avocado Lettuce Wraps

Total Time: 15 minutes

Preparation Time: 15 minutes

Serves: 3

Ingredients:

- 1 lb ground turkey

- 1 teaspoon taco seasoning

- Lettuce leaves for wrapping

- 1 avocado, sliced

- Salsa (low-carb)

Instructions:

1. Brown the ground turkey in a skillet and add taco spice.

2. Arrange the leaves of lettuce onto a dish.

3. Spoon each leaf with ground turkey.

4. Add salsa and avocado slices on top.

5. Enjoy after wrapping!

6. Details about Nutrition (per serving):

7. 280 calories, 20g of protein, 20g of fat, 6g of carbohydrates, and 3g of fiber

22. Broccoli and Cheddar Soup

Total Time: 30 minutes

Cooking Time: 20 minutes

Serves: 4

Ingredients:

- 4 cups broccoli florets

- 2 cups chicken broth

- 1 cup heavy cream

- 2 cups shredded cheddar cheese

- Salt and pepper to taste

Instructions:

1. Bring the chicken stock to a boil in a pot.

2. Simmer the broccoli florets until they are soft.

3. Smoothly blend the soup.

4. Turn the heat back on and mix in the cheddar cheese and heavy cream.

5. Once the cheese has melted, season with salt and pepper and boil.

6. Details about Nutrition (per serving):

7. 300 calories; 15g of protein; 25g of fat; 8g of carbohydrates; and 3g of fiber

Easy Ingredients & Simple Instruction

1. Grilled Chicken Caesar Salad

Total Time: 20 minutes

Cooking Time: 15 minutes

Serves: 2

Ingredients:

- 2 boneless, skinless chicken breasts

- 1 tablespoon olive oil

- Salt and pepper to taste

- Romaine lettuce

- Caesar dressing (low-carb)

Instructions:

1. Use salt and pepper to season the chicken.

2. Cook chicken on an olive oil grill until it's done.

3. Serve the grilled chicken with its slices on top of a bed of romaine lettuce.

4. Pour in some reduced-carb Caesar dressing.

2. Zucchini Noodles with Pesto

Total Time: 15 minutes

Cooking Time: 10 minutes

Serves: 2

Ingredients:

- 2 medium-sized zucchinis

- 1 cup fresh basil leaves

- 1/4 cup pine nuts

- 1/2 cup grated Parmesan cheese

- 1/3 cup olive oil

- Salt and pepper to taste

Instructions:

1. Turn zucchini noodles into spirals.

2. Blend together basil, pine nuts, Parmesan, and olive oil in a blender. Process till smooth.

3. Combine pesto sauce with zoodles.

4. Add pepper and salt for seasoning.

3. Baked Salmon with Lemon Butter

Total Time: 25 minutes

Cooking Time: 15 minutes

Serves: 2

Ingredients:

- 2 salmon fillets

- 2 tablespoons melted butter

- 1 lemon (juiced)

- Garlic powder, salt, and pepper to taste

Instructions:

1. Turn the oven on to 400°F, or 200°C.

2. Arrange the fish onto a baking tray.

3. Add salt, pepper, garlic powder, lemon juice, and melted butter.

4. Apply the blend onto the fish.

5. Bake the salmon for 15 minutes, or until it is thoroughly cooked.

4. Cauliflower Mash

Total Time: 20 minutes

Cooking Time: 15 minutes

Serves: 4

Ingredients:

- 1 head of cauliflower

- 2 cloves garlic (minced)

- 2 tablespoons butter

- Salt and pepper to taste

- Chopped chives for garnish

Instructions:

1. Tenderize cauliflower by steaming or boiling it.

2. Add butter, garlic, salt, and pepper to mashed cauliflower.

3. Sprinkle chopped chives over top.

5. Egg Salad Lettuce Wraps

Total Time: 15 minutes

Cooking Time: 10 minutes

Serves: 2

Ingredients:

- 4 hard-boiled eggs (chopped)

- 1/4 cup mayonnaise (sugar-free)

- 1 teaspoon Dijon mustard

- Salt and pepper to taste

- Lettuce leaves for wrapping

Instructions:

1. Combine chopped eggs, mustard, mayonnaise, pepper, and salt.

2. Ladle the egg salad over a leaf of lettuce.

3. Use toothpicks to secure the wrapping.

6. Shrimp Stir-Fry

Total Time: 20 minutes

Cooking Time: 10 minutes

Serves: 2

Ingredients:

- 1 pound shrimp (peeled and deveined)

- 2 cups broccoli florets

- 1 bell pepper (sliced)

- 2 tablespoons soy sauce (low-carb)

- 1 tablespoon sesame oil

- Garlic powder and ginger to taste

Instructions:

1. Sesame oil is heated in a pan.

2. Add bell pepper, broccoli, and shrimp.

3. Stir-fry the vegetables and prawns until they are soft and pink.

4. Add ginger, garlic powder, and soy sauce for seasoning.

7. Avocado and Bacon Stuffed Mushrooms

Total Time: 25 minutes

Cooking Time: 15 minutes

Serves: 4

Ingredients:

- 8 large mushrooms (stems removed)

- 1 avocado (mashed)

- 4 slices cooked bacon (crumbled)

- 1/4 cup shredded cheese

- Salt and pepper to taste

Instructions:

1. Turn the oven on to 375°F, or 190°C.

2. Combine shredded cheese, crumbled bacon, and mashed avocado.

3. Stuff mixture into mushrooms.

4. Bake for fifteen minutes.

8. Beef and Broccoli Skillet

Total Time: 30 minutes

Cooking Time: 20 minutes

Serves: 4

Ingredients:

- 1 pound beef sirloin (sliced)

- 2 cups broccoli florets

- 2 tablespoons soy sauce (low-carb)

- 1 tablespoon olive oil

- Garlic powder and ginger to taste

Instructions:

1. Olive oil is heated in a skillet.

2. Cook the beef until it turns brown.

3. Stir in ginger, garlic powder, soy sauce, and broccoli.

4. Stir broccoli till it becomes soft.

9. Cucumber and Feta Salad

Total Time: 15 minutes

Cooking Time: 0 minutes

Serves: 2

Ingredients:

- 2 cucumbers (sliced)
- 1/2 cup feta cheese (crumbled)
- 2 tablespoons olive oil
- 1 tablespoon red wine vinegar
- Salt and pepper to taste

Instructions:

1. Cucumber slices and feta should be combined in a bowl.
2. Add a drizzle of red wine vinegar and olive oil.
3. Add pepper and salt for seasoning.

10. Eggplant Lasagna

Total Time: 45 minutes

Cooking Time: 30 minutes

Serves: 6

Ingredients:

- 1 large eggplant (sliced)
- 1 pound ground beef
- 1 cup low-carb marinara sauce
- 1 cup ricotta cheese
- 1 cup shredded mozzarella
- Italian seasoning, salt, and pepper to taste

Instructions:

1. Turn the oven on to 375°F, or 190°C.

2. Add salt, pepper, and Italian seasoning to brown ground beef.

3. Arrange the beef, mozzarella, ricotta, marinara, and sliced eggplant in a baking dish.

4. After 30 minutes of baking, repeat the layers.

11. Spinach and Feta Stuffed Chicken

Total Time: 30 minutes

Cooking Time: 20 minutes

Serves: 2

Ingredients:

- 2 boneless, skinless chicken breasts

- 1 cup fresh spinach (chopped)

- 1/2 cup feta cheese (crumbled)

- 1 tablespoon olive oil

- Garlic powder, salt, and pepper to taste

Instructions:

1. Turn the oven on to 375°F, or 190°C.

2. On each of the chicken breasts, cut a pocket.

3. Combine feta, spinach, salt, pepper, and garlic powder.

4. Stuff the mixture inside each chicken breast.

5. Roast in olive oil for 20 minutes after searing.

12. Broccoli Cheddar Soup

Total Time: 30 minutes

Cooking Time: 20 minutes

Serves: 4

Ingredients:

- 2 cups broccoli florets
- 1 cup cheddar cheese (shredded)
- 2 cups chicken broth
- 1 cup heavy cream
- Salt and pepper to taste

Instructions:

1. Broccoli should be steamed until soft.
2. Puree broccoli, heavy cream, and chicken broth in a blender until smooth.
3. Transfer mixture to a pot, stir in cheddar cheese, and cook over medium heat until cheese melts.
4. Add pepper and salt for seasoning.

13. Turkey and Avocado Lettuce Wraps
Total Time: 15 minutes

Cooking Time: 10 minutes

Serves: 2

Ingredients:

- 1/2 pound ground turkey
- 1 teaspoon cumin
- 1 teaspoon chili powder

- Lettuce leaves for wrapping

- 1 avocado (sliced)

- Salsa (sugar-free)

Instructions:

1. Add the chili powder and cumin to the ground turkey and cook until browned.

2. Place turkey onto a bed of lettuce.

3. Add salsa and sliced avocado on top.

14. Lemon Garlic Shrimp Skewers

Total Time: 20 minutes

Cooking Time: 10 minutes

Serves: 2

Ingredients:

- 1/2 pound shrimp (peeled and deveined)

- 2 tablespoons olive oil

- Zest and juice of 1 lemon

- 2 cloves garlic (minced)

- Salt and pepper to taste

Instructions:

1. Heat a grill pan or grill.

2. Shrimp, olive oil, lemon zest, lemon juice, garlic, salt, and pepper should all be combined in a bowl.

3. Put shrimp on skewers and cook them for three to four minutes on each side.

15. Caesar Chicken Lettuce Wraps

Total Time: 25 minutes

Cooking Time: 20 minutes

Serves: 2

Ingredients:

- 2 boneless, skinless chicken breasts

- 1 tablespoon olive oil

- Caesar dressing (low-carb)

- Romaine lettuce leaves

- Parmesan cheese (shaved)

Instructions:

1. Use salt and pepper to season the chicken.

2. Cook chicken on an olive oil grill until it's done.

3. Cut up chicken and stuff it between lettuce leaves.

4. Top with shaved Parmesan and drizzle with low-carb Caesar dressing.

16. Cabbage and Sausage Stir-Fry

Total Time: 25 minutes

Cooking Time: 15 minutes

Serves: 4

Ingredients:

- 1/2 head cabbage (shredded)
- 1 pound sausage (sliced)
- 1 onion (sliced)
- 2 cloves garlic (minced)
- 2 tablespoons soy sauce (low-carb)

Instructions:

1. Sausage should be cooked in a big skillet until browned.
2. Add the garlic and onions and sauté until tender.
3. Stir-fry the shredded cabbage with soy sauce until it becomes soft.

17. Caprese Salad Skewers

Total Time: 15 minutes

Cooking Time: 0 minutes

Serves: 4

Ingredients:

- Cherry tomatoes
- Fresh mozzarella balls
- Fresh basil leaves
- Balsamic glaze
- Salt and pepper to taste

Instructions:

1. Put basil, mozzarella balls, and cherry tomatoes on skewers.

2. Pour balsamic glaze over.

3. Add pepper and salt for seasoning.

18. Portobello Mushroom Pizzas

Total Time: 30 minutes

Cooking Time: 20 minutes

Serves: 2

Ingredients:

- 4 large Portobello mushrooms

- 1/2 cup low-carb marinara sauce

- 1 cup shredded mozzarella cheese

- 1/4 cup sliced pepperoni

- Italian seasoning to taste

Instructions:

1. Turn the oven on to 375°F, or 190°C.

2. Take off the mushroom stems and stuff them with cheese, pepperoni, and sauce.

3. Bake until the cheese is bubbling, about 20 minutes.

4. Add a dash of Italian spice.

19. Cilantro Lime Chicken Skillet

Total Time: 30 minutes

Cooking Time: 20 minutes

Serves: 4

Ingredients:

- 1 pound chicken thighs (boneless, skinless)
- 1 tablespoon olive oil
- Juice of 2 limes
- 1/4 cup fresh cilantro (chopped)
- Cumin, garlic powder, salt, and pepper to taste

Instructions:

1. Garlic powder, cumin, salt, and pepper are used to season chicken.
2. Heat up some olive oil in a skillet and sear the chicken till browned.
3. Drizzle chicken with lime juice and garnish with cilantro.

20. Greek Salad with Grilled Chicken

Total Time: 25 minutes

Cooking Time: 15 minutes

Serves: 2

Ingredients:

- 2 boneless, skinless chicken breasts
- 1 tablespoon olive oil
- 1 cucumber (sliced)
- Cherry tomatoes
- Kalamata olives
- Feta cheese (crumbled)
- Greek dressing (low-carb)

Instructions:

1. Use salt and pepper to season the chicken.

2. Cook chicken on an olive oil grill until it's done.

3. Serve the sliced chicken over a bed of tomatoes, cucumbers, feta, and olives.

4. Drizzle with Greek dressing reduced in carbs.

Servings Info & Cooking Times

Recipe 1: Grilled Lemon Garlic Chicken

Total Time: 30 minutes

Cooking Time: 20 minutes

Serves: 4

Ingredients:

- 4 boneless, skinless chicken breasts

- 2 lemons (juiced and zested)

- 3 cloves garlic (minced)

- 2 tablespoons olive oil

- Salt and pepper to taste

Instructions:

1. Set the grill's temperature to medium-high.

2. Combine the lemon juice, zest, minced garlic, olive oil, salt, and pepper in a small bowl.

3. Use the lemon-garlic mixture to lightly coat the chicken breasts.

4. The chicken should be cooked through after about ten minutes on each side of the grill.

5. Warm up the food.

Recipe 2: Zucchini Noodles with Pesto

Total Time: 15 minutes

Cooking Time: 10 minutes

Serves: 2

Ingredients:

- 2 large zucchinis (spiralized into noodles)

- 1 cup fresh basil leaves

- 1/4 cup pine nuts

- 1/2 cup grated Parmesan cheese

- 2 cloves garlic

- 1/2 cup olive oil

- Salt and pepper to taste

Instructions:

1. Put the garlic, basil, pine nuts, Parmesan, salt, and pepper in a food processor. Pulse until chopped finely.

2. Add the olive oil gradually while the machine is running and mix thoroughly.

3. Sauté zucchini noodles for five to seven minutes on medium heat in a pan.

4. Combine the pesto and zucchini noodles, tossing to coat evenly.

5. Warm up and serve.

Recipe 3: Broccoli and Cheddar Stuffed Chicken

Total Time: 40 minutes

Cooking Time: 25 minutes

Serves: 3

Ingredients:

- 3 boneless, skinless chicken breasts
- 1 cup steamed broccoli (chopped)
- 1 cup shredded cheddar cheese
- 1 teaspoon garlic powder
- Salt and pepper to taste

Instructions:

1. Turn the oven on to 375°F, or 190°C.
2. On each of the chicken breasts, cut a pocket.
3. Combine the chopped broccoli, cheddar cheese, salt, pepper, and garlic powder in a bowl.
4. Place a filling of the broccoli and cheddar mixture inside each chicken breast.
5. Bake the chicken for 20 to 25 minutes, or until it is thoroughly done.

Recipe 4: Caesar Salad with Grilled Shrimp

Total Time: 25 minutes

Cooking Time: 10 minutes

Serves: 2

Ingredients:

- 1 lb large shrimp, peeled and deveined
- 2 tablespoons olive oil
- 1 teaspoon garlic powder
- Salt and pepper to taste
- Romaine lettuce, chopped
- Caesar dressing (low-carb)
- Grated Parmesan cheese

Instructions:

1. Toss shrimp with olive oil, salt, pepper, and garlic powder in a bowl.
2. Grill shrimp until opaque, 2 to 3 minutes per side.
3. Place sliced romaine on plates and add grilled shrimp on top.
4. After adding a drizzle of Caesar dressing, top with Parmesan cheese.

Recipe 5: Eggplant Lasagna

Total Time: 1 hour

Cooking Time: 45 minutes

Serves: 6

Ingredients:

- 1 large eggplant, thinly sliced lengthwise
- 1 lb ground beef or turkey
- 2 cups low-carb marinara sauce
- 1 cup ricotta cheese

- 1 cup shredded mozzarella cheese
- 1/2 cup grated Parmesan cheese
- Fresh basil for garnish

Instructions:

1. Turn the oven on to 375°F, or 190°C.

2. Grill each side of the eggplant slices for two minutes.

3. Brown the ground meat in a skillet and then pour in the marinara sauce.

4. Arrange the eggplant, meat sauce, mozzarella, and ricotta in a baking dish. Repeat.

5. After adding some Parmesan cheese, bake for thirty minutes.

6. Add some fresh basil as a garnish before serving.

Recipe 6: Spinach and Feta Stuffed Mushrooms

Total Time: 30 minutes

Cooking Time: 15 minutes

Serves: 4

Ingredients:

- 16 large mushrooms, stems removed
- 2 cups fresh spinach, chopped
- 1/2 cup crumbled feta cheese
- 2 cloves garlic, minced
- 2 tablespoons olive oil
- Salt and pepper to taste

Instructions:

1. Set oven temperature to 175°C/350°F.

2. Garlic and spinach should be sautéed in olive oil in a pan until wilted.

3. Add the feta, salt, and pepper to the spinach.

4. Insert the spinach and feta mixture into the caps of the mushrooms.

5. Bake the mushrooms for 15 minutes, or until they are soft.

Recipe 7: Salmon with Dill Sauce

Total Time: 20 minutes

Cooking Time: 15 minutes

Serves: 2

Ingredients:

-   2 salmon fillets

-   2 tablespoons olive oil

-   1 tablespoon fresh dill, chopped

-   1 tablespoon lemon juice

-   Salt and pepper to taste

Instructions:

1. Set oven temperature to 400°F, or 200°C.

2. Salmon fillets should be put on a baking pan.

3. Add a drizzle of olive oil and season with salt, pepper, lemon juice, and chopped dill.

4. Bake for 12 to 15 minutes, or until a fork can easily pierce the salmon.

Recipe 8: Cauliflower Fried Rice

Total Time: 25 minutes

Cooking Time: 15 minutes

Serves: 4

Ingredients:

- 1 medium cauliflower, grated

- 2 tablespoons sesame oil

- 1 cup mixed vegetables (peas, carrots, bell peppers)

- 2 eggs, beaten

- 3 tablespoons soy sauce (low-carb)

- Green onions for garnish

Instructions:

1. Sesame oil should be heated over medium heat in a big skillet.

2. Sauté the grated cauliflower for five to seven minutes.

3. Arrange the cauliflower aside and use the vacant space to scramble eggs.

4. Combine eggs and cauliflower, whisk with soy sauce and add mixed vegetables.

5. After five more minutes of cooking, add some green onions as a garnish.

Recipe 9: Avocado and Bacon Wrapped Chicken

Total Time: 40 minutes

Cooking Time: 25 minutes

Serves: 3

Ingredients:

- 3 boneless, skinless chicken breasts

- 1 ripe avocado, sliced

- 6 slices bacon

- Salt and pepper to taste

- Toothpicks

Instructions:

1. Turn the oven on to 375°F, or 190°C.

2. Add salt and pepper to chicken breasts for seasoning.

3. Top each chicken breast with a slice of avocado and cover with bacon.

4. Put toothpicks in to secure, then bake for 20 to 25 minutes.

Recipe 10: Cabbage and Sausage Skillet

Total Time: 30 minutes

Cooking Time: 20 minutes

Serves: 4

Ingredients:

- 1 lb smoked sausage, sliced

- 1 small head of cabbage, shredded

- 1 onion, thinly sliced

- 2 cloves garlic, minced

- 2 tablespoons olive oil

- Salt and pepper to taste

Instructions:

1. Heat the olive oil in a big skillet over medium heat.

2. After adding, sauté the sausage slices until browned.

3. Add the garlic and onions and sauté until tender.

4. Add the shreds of cabbage and heat through.

5. Add salt and pepper for seasoning, then serve warm.

Recipe 11: Cheesy Bacon Wrapped Asparagus

Total Time: 25 minutes

Cooking Time: 15 minutes

Serves: 4

Ingredients:

- 1 lb fresh asparagus spears

- 8 slices bacon

- 1/2 cup shredded cheddar cheese

- Olive oil for drizzling

- Salt and pepper to taste

Instructions:

1. Set oven temperature to 400°F, or 200°C.

2. After cutting off the tough ends, divide the asparagus into bundles.

3. Arrange each bundle on a baking sheet after securing it with a slice of bacon.

4. Add a drizzle of olive oil and season with pepper and salt.

5. Bake until bacon is crispy, about 15 minutes.

6. Add some shredded cheddar cheese on top, then bake for a further two to three minutes, or until the cheese is melted.

Recipe 12: Spaghetti Squash with Meatballs

Total Time: 45 minutes

Cooking Time: 30 minutes

Serves: 4

Ingredients:

- 1 medium spaghetti squash

- 1 lb ground beef or turkey

- 1 cup low-carb marinara sauce

- 1/2 cup grated Parmesan cheese

- 1 teaspoon Italian seasoning

- Salt and pepper to taste

- Fresh basil for garnish

Instructions:

1. Set oven temperature to 400°F, or 200°C.

2. Scoop out the seeds after cutting the spaghetti squash in half lengthwise.

3. Squash halves should be placed cut side down on a baking pan and baked for thirty minutes.

4. Ground meat should be browned in a skillet before adding marinara sauce, salt, pepper, and Italian seasoning.

5. Using a fork, scrape the cooked spaghetti squash to make "noodles."

6. Place the meatball mixture on top, then top with Parmesan and fresh basil.

Recipe 13: Creamy Garlic Parmesan Brussels Sprouts

Total Time: 25 minutes

Cooking Time: 15 minutes

Serves: 4

Ingredients:

- 1 lb Brussels sprouts, trimmed and halved

- 2 tablespoons olive oil

- 3 cloves garlic, minced

- 1/2 cup heavy cream

- 1/2 cup grated Parmesan cheese

- Salt and pepper to taste

Instructions:

1. Warm up the olive oil in a big skillet over medium heat.

2. Brussels sprouts should be added and sautéed until just browned.

3. Cook the minced garlic for one to two more minutes after adding it.

4. Add the heavy cream and stir continuously until the mixture starts to thicken.

5. Add the salt, pepper, and Parmesan cheese and stir.

6. Cook until the Brussels sprouts are soft and the sauce is creamy, about 3 to 4 more minutes.

Recipe 14: Lemon Herb Grilled Swordfish

Total Time: 30 minutes

Cooking Time: 15 minutes

Serves: 2

Ingredients:

- 2 swordfish steaks

- Zest and juice of 1 lemon

- 2 tablespoons fresh parsley, chopped

- 1 tablespoon olive oil

- 2 cloves garlic, minced

- Salt and pepper to taste

Instructions:

1. Set the grill's temperature to medium-high.

2. Combine the lemon zest, lemon juice, minced garlic, olive oil, chopped parsley, salt, and pepper in a bowl.

3. Apply the lemon-herb mixture to the swordfish steaks.

4. The swordfish should be cooked through after grilling for 7 to 8 minutes on each side.

5. Accompany with a lemon wedge.

Recipe 15: Avocado and Tuna Salad

Total Time: 15 minutes

Preparation Time: 15 minutes

Serves: 2

Ingredients:

- 1 can (5 oz) tuna, drained
- 1 avocado, diced
- 1/4 cup red onion, finely chopped
- 1/4 cup celery, chopped
- 2 tablespoons mayonnaise
- 1 tablespoon Dijon mustard
- Salt and pepper to taste
- Lettuce leaves for serving

Instructions:

1. Tuna, diced avocado, chopped red onion, and celery should all be combined in a bowl.
2. Combine mayonnaise, Dijon mustard, pepper, and salt in a small bowl.
3. After adding the dressing to the tuna mixture, gently toss to mix.
4. Place a bed of lettuce leaves on which to serve the tuna salad.

Recipe 16: Portobello Mushroom Pizzas

Total Time: 25 minutes

Cooking Time: 15 minutes

Serves: 2

Ingredients:

- 4 large portobello mushroom caps

- 1/2 cup sugar-free marinara sauce

- 1 cup shredded mozzarella cheese

- 1/4 cup sliced pepperoni or cooked sausage (optional)

- Fresh basil for garnish

- Olive oil for drizzling

- Salt and pepper to taste

Instructions:

1. Set oven temperature to 400°F, or 200°C.

2. Take off the stems and clean the mushroom caps.

3. The mushrooms should be put, gill side up, on a baking sheet.

4. Drizzle each cap with marinara sauce, then add desired toppings and cheese on top.

5. Add a drizzle of olive oil and season with pepper and salt.

6. Bake the cheese for fifteen minutes, or until it is bubbling and melted.

7. Add some fresh basil as a garnish before serving.

Recipe 17: Greek Salad with Grilled Chicken

Total Time: 30 minutes

Cooking Time: 15 minutes

Serves: 2

Ingredients:

- 2 boneless, skinless chicken breasts
- 1 teaspoon dried oregano
- 1 teaspoon dried basil
- Salt and pepper to taste
- 2 tablespoons olive oil (for chicken)
- Mixed salad greens
- Cherry tomatoes, halved
- Cucumber, sliced
- Kalamata olives
- Feta cheese, crumbled
- Greek dressing (low-carb)

Instructions:

1. Season chicken breasts with salt, pepper, oregano, and basil.
2. In a grill pan, heat the olive oil over medium-high heat.
3. Cook the chicken on the grill for 6–7 minutes on each side, or until done.
4. Combine the cucumber, olives, feta, cherry tomatoes, and salad greens in a big bowl.
5. Arrange the grilled chicken slices over the salad.
6. Before serving, toss with a drizzle of Greek dressing.

Recipe 18: Cauliflower and Broccoli Casserole
Total Time: 40 minutes

Cooking Time: 25 minutes

Serves: 4

Ingredients:

- 1 small head cauliflower, cut into florets

- 1 small head broccoli, cut into florets

- 1/2 cup heavy cream

- 1 cup shredded cheddar cheese

- 2 tablespoons cream cheese

- 1 teaspoon Dijon mustard

- Salt and pepper to taste

- 1/4 cup grated Parmesan cheese

Instructions:

1. Turn the oven on to 375°F, or 190°C.

2. Broccoli and cauliflower should be steamed until barely soft.

3. Heat the heavy cream, cheddar, cream, Dijon mustard, salt, and pepper in a saucepan until they become smooth.

4. Transfer the cheese sauce-mixed steamed veggies to a baking dish.

5. Top with Parmesan cheese and bake for 20 to 25 minutes, or until brown and bubbling.

Recipe 19: Turkey and Veggie Skewers

Total Time: 30 minutes

Cooking Time: 15 minutes

Serves: 4

Ingredients:

- 1 lb turkey breast, cut into cubes
- 1 zucchini, sliced
- 1 bell pepper, cut into chunks
- 1 red onion, cut into wedges
- 2 tablespoons olive oil
- 1 teaspoon dried thyme
- Salt and pepper to taste
- Wooden skewers, soaked in water

Instructions:

1. Turn the heat up to medium-high on the grill or grill pan.
2. Stuff the wet skewers with bell pepper, red onion, zucchini, and turkey.
3. Combine the olive oil, salt, pepper, and dried thyme in a small bowl.
4. Apply the olive oil mixture to the skewers.
5. Cook the turkey for 10 to 12 minutes, rotating it once or twice, or until the vegetables are soft and cooked through.

Recipe 20: Spinach and Bacon Stuffed Chicken

Total Time: 40 minutes

Cooking Time: 25 minutes

Serves: 3

Ingredients:

- 3 boneless, skinless chicken breasts

- 1 cup fresh spinach, chopped

- 1/2 cup cream cheese

- 1/4 cup cooked and crumbled bacon

- 1 teaspoon garlic powder

- Salt and pepper to taste

- Toothpicks

Instructions:

1. Turn the oven on to 375°F, or 190°C.

2. Combine the cream cheese, bacon, chopped spinach, garlic powder, salt, and pepper in a bowl.

3. To make a pocket, cut a horizontal slit in each chicken breast.

4. Place a filling of the spinach and bacon mixture inside each chicken breast.

5. Put toothpicks in to secure, then bake for 20 to 25 minutes, or until chicken is thoroughly done.

Recipe 21: Shrimp and Avocado Salad

Total Time: 20 minutes

Preparation Time: 15 minutes

Serves: 2

Ingredients:

- 1 lb shrimp, peeled and deveined

- 1 avocado, diced

- 1 cup cherry tomatoes, halved

- 1/4 cup red onion, finely chopped

- 2 tablespoons fresh cilantro, chopped

- 1 lime, juiced

- 2 tablespoons olive oil

- Salt and pepper to taste

Instructions:

1. Cook the shrimp in a skillet over medium-high heat until they become opaque and pink.

2. Cooked shrimp, chopped avocado, cherry tomatoes, red onion, and cilantro should all be combined in a big bowl.

3. Mix the lime juice, olive oil, salt, and pepper in a small bowl.

4. After adding the dressing to the shrimp mixture, gently toss to mix.

5. Present cold.

Recipe 22: Egg and Vegetable Breakfast Muffins

Total Time: 30 minutes

Cooking Time: 20 minutes

Serves: 6

Ingredients:

- 6 eggs

- 1/2 cup bell peppers, diced

- 1/2 cup spinach, chopped

- 1/4 cup red onion, finely chopped

- 1/4 cup grated cheddar cheese

- Salt and pepper to taste

Instructions:

1. Turn the oven on to 375°F, or 190°C.

2. Beat eggs, bell peppers, spinach, red onion, salt, and pepper in a bowl.

3. After greasing a muffin tin, divide the egg mixture equally among the cups.

4. Top with grated cheddar cheese.

5. Bake the eggs for 18 to 20 minutes, or until they set.

6. Before taking the muffins out of the tin, let them cool somewhat.

Recipe 23: Lemon Garlic Roasted Brussels Sprouts

Total Time: 35 minutes

Cooking Time: 25 minutes

Serves: 4

Ingredients:

- 1 lb Brussels sprouts, trimmed and halved

- 2 tablespoons olive oil

- 2 cloves garlic, minced

- Zest and juice of 1 lemon

- Salt and pepper to taste

- 2 tablespoons grated Parmesan cheese (optional)

Instructions:

1. Set oven temperature to 400°F, or 200°C.

2. Brussels sprouts should be tossed with olive oil, salt, pepper, lemon zest, and juice.

3. Arrange them on a baking sheet in a single layer.

4. Roast the Brussels sprouts for 25 minutes, or until they are crispy and golden brown.

5. Before serving, top with grated Parmesan cheese, if preferred.

Recipe 24: Cucumber and Smoked Salmon Roll-Ups

Total Time: 15 minutes

Preparation Time: 15 minutes

Serves: 2

Ingredients:

- 1 large cucumber
- 4 oz smoked salmon
- 1/4 cup cream cheese
- 2 tablespoons capers
- Fresh dill for garnish
- Lemon wedges

Instructions:

1. Cut the cucumber lengthwise into thin strips with a vegetable peeler.

2. Apply a thin coating of cream cheese onto every strip of cucumber.

3. Put a smoked salmon slice over the cream cheese.

4. Drizzle the fish with capers.

5. Use toothpicks to secure the cucumber strips as you roll them up.

6. Serve with lemon wedges and garnish with fresh dill.

Recipe 25: Grilled Asparagus with Lemon Butter

Total Time: 20 minutes

Cooking Time: 10 minutes

Serves: 4

Ingredients:

- 1 lb fresh asparagus, trimmed
- 2 tablespoons olive oil
- Salt and pepper to taste
- Zest and juice of 1 lemon
- 2 tablespoons unsalted butter, melted

Instructions:

1. Set the grill's temperature to medium-high.
2. Add salt, pepper, and olive oil to asparagus spears and toss.
3. Grill the asparagus for 5 to 7 minutes, turning it from time to time, until it becomes soft and slightly browned.
4. Combine lemon juice and zest with melted butter in a small bowl.
5. Before serving, drizzle the grilled asparagus with the lemon butter.

Made in the USA
Columbia, SC
18 November 2024

46958962R00104